Laurence McGowan, *stoneware vase*

Christine Jones, *colorful vessels*

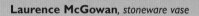

John Leach, *stoneware clay*

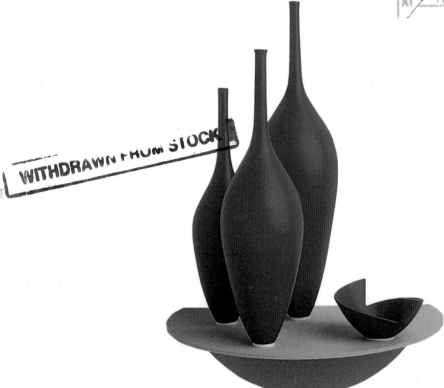

THE
POTTER'S
PRIMER

Duncan Ross, *burnished bowl*

THE POTTER'S PRIMER

Morgen Hall

APPLE

A QUARTO BOOK

Published by The Apple Press
The Old Brewery
6 Blundell Street
London N7 9BH

Copyright © 1997

ISBN 1-85076-976-1

This book was designed and produced by:
Quarto Publishing plc
The Old Brewery
6 Blundell Street
London N7 9BH

Senior editor Kate Kirby
Senior art editor/Designer Julie Francis
Copy editor Hazel Harrison, Jean Coppendale
Photographers Charles and Patricia Aithie,
Les Weiss
Editorial Director Pippa Rubinstein
Art director Moira Clinch

Typeset by Central Southern Typesetters,
Eastbourne
Manufactured by Universal Graphics Pte Ltd
in Singapore
Printed by Star Standard in Singapore

Publisher's Note
Pottery can be dangerous. Always follow the
instructions carefully, and exercise caution.
Follow the safety procedures accompanying
the techniques.
As far as the methods and techniques
mentioned in this book are concerned, all
statements, information, and advice given here
are believed to be accurate. However, neither
the author, copyright holder, nor the publisher
can accept any legal liability.

CONTENTS

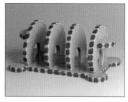

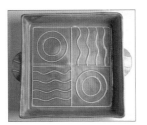

INTRODUCTION

Peter Meanley *"Salt glazed" teapot, thrown with press molded additions.*

Clay is a magic material. It is extremely enjoyable to work with, and it is one of the world's most versatile substances. Clay and glaze, fired to temperatures high enough to produce ceramic, can create almost any shape, texture, color, or pattern imaginable. This fusing together of earth's materials can produce gem-like qualities, making the exploration of ceramics a grand alchemy.

The versatility of ceramics has been celebrated throughout the world for thousands of years, creating a rich history which reflects the ideas and experiences of the makers.

Because the boundaries are so wide, indeed almost limitless, it can be daunting to begin working with ceramics. This book is intended as a starting point, giving you a series of step-by-step projects showing many basic making techniques, which you can then take further to develop your own work.

WHERE TO FIND MORE INFORMATION

Ceramics is too vast a subject for any single book to cover fully, so you will also need to gather in all other forms of help and information available. One of the best sources will often be from your ceramic materials suppliers. They produce catalogues of their materials which usually have important health and safety information. You should also ensure that you receive full working instructions for any equipment you buy. Many people enjoy taking pottery classes. These can provide an important source of technical help as well as a creative and sociable time, though it can be frustrating to find you are limited to only two or three hours a week. Most art colleges have ceramics courses which provide excellent full-time instruction, and there are also many short pottery courses run by working potters. A one- or two-week holiday learning pottery from a professional in their own workshop can be one of the best ways to enjoy

Susanne Altzweig *Thrown jugs, press-molded plate, tin glazed with majolica decoration.*

Ray Finch *"Salt fired" bowl with stem foot, thrown with slip decoration.*

learning. Ask your ceramics supplier if they know of any potters running workshops in your area, or you can find them listed in the classified ads of many ceramic magazines.

National crafts councils also provide a mine of information including the addresses of ceramics magazines, as well as those of potters who welcome visitors to their studios. Buying hand-made ceramics from craft galleries or direct from the makers provides a wealth of information and inspiration.

Museums and libraries are a valuable source of information on ceramics, as is the Internet. There are also many potters' associations that provide a network of support including pottery demonstration days and other events.

Face mask with filters.

HEALTH AND SAFETY

If you are going to set up a workshop in your home, you will need to consider all of the practical and safety implications. Ask your pottery teacher and/or suppliers of equipment for advice. The following are some of the hazards to be aware of.

• Due to the toxic nature of some of the materials used, as well as the dust created by dry clay, you should *not* try to work in the kitchen of your home. You will need to have an unused, well-lit room which should ideally be on the ground floor to make the moving in of equipment and materials easier.

• Your kiln should be sited in a separate unused room, unless you have a fumes extractor installed. Ensure the extractor and its installation are designed to cope with the high temperatures of the kiln fumes, otherwise it will be a fire hazard. Care must also be taken to ensure that the kiln will not be a fire hazard. Ask your kiln supplier or even the local fire department for advice before installing your kiln and extractor.

• The extremely high temperatures reached by kilns make them potentially lethal if their doors are opened during the firing. Even the outsides of kilns become extremely hot during firing, so children and animals should not be allowed near firing kilns unsupervised. Locks can be put onto kiln doors, or the kiln room itself could be kept locked. Children must *never* be allowed to play with kilns, even when switched off and cold, as they could become trapped or injured.

• The room will need to have a sink with running water, or easy access to one. Take care never to wash clay, glaze or plaster down the sink, however.

• All potteries need plenty of shelving to free the working surfaces for making. The types of shelving which have removable supports to give adjustable heights are the most useful, as these allow for different sizes of work.

• Most of the colorants and many of the glazes used in ceramics are *toxic* until they are safely fired to form a glassy surface. Some materials remain toxic in certain glazes even after the glaze firing (see hazard warning information on page 18). Extreme care must therefore be taken to not inhale or ingest any of these materials. Face masks with suitable dust filters *must* be worn whenever handling powdered materials. Care must be taken to not contaminate food or drink. Children must always be carefully supervised when they are using toxic materials.

• Dry clay dust is mostly silica. Silica dust should not be inhaled as this can have cumulative effects which cause silicosis, a lung disease. Glaze dust also contains silica, as well as other potentially toxic materials, so glaze dust must not be inhaled or ingested.

• To keep dust down, the work surfaces should be sponged clean and the floor of your pottery workshop mopped clean every day; never brush the floor as this makes dust airborne. Carpets are unsuitable for pottery floors.

If in doubt about any safety aspect of making or using ceramics, always seek further advice from the suppliers of the materials or equipment.

Making ceramics can be a completely safe activity, as shown by the large number of full-time potters who live long and healthy lives. Take care to find out about the materials and equipment you buy and how to use them safely, and the world of ceramics is there for you to enjoy exploring.

TOOLS & EQUIPMENT

1 Hardwood modeling tool
2 Hardwood modeling tool
3 Forged steel tool (used for carving plaster detail)
4 Tapered hole cutter. The taper allows you to cut holes of different sizes to suit different pots
5 Coil-maker tool, available in different sizes
6 Double-ended strip-turning tool. Different shapes at each end enables a wider range of shapes to be turned
7 Small double-ended strip-turning tool
8 Sgraffito tool for scratch decoration
9 Potter's knife, one of the most useful tools in the pottery

10 Clay gun: small clay extruder with a selection of different die plates for extruding small lengths of clay which can be used, for example, as decorative inlay
11 Slip trailer (rubber bulb)
12 Slip trailer (plastic bottle)
13 Wooden rolling pin. Extra-long rolling pins are especially useful for rolling out slabs of clay
14 Cutting wire
15 Doubled twisted cutting wire. Will leave a decorative rippled surface on the cut clay
16 Cup sieve 120 mesh, used for sieving small amounts of slip, glaze stains or glazes
17 Large lawn sieve, 120 mesh, for sieving large amounts of slips or glazes
18 Large and small rubber kidneys, available stiff or flexible

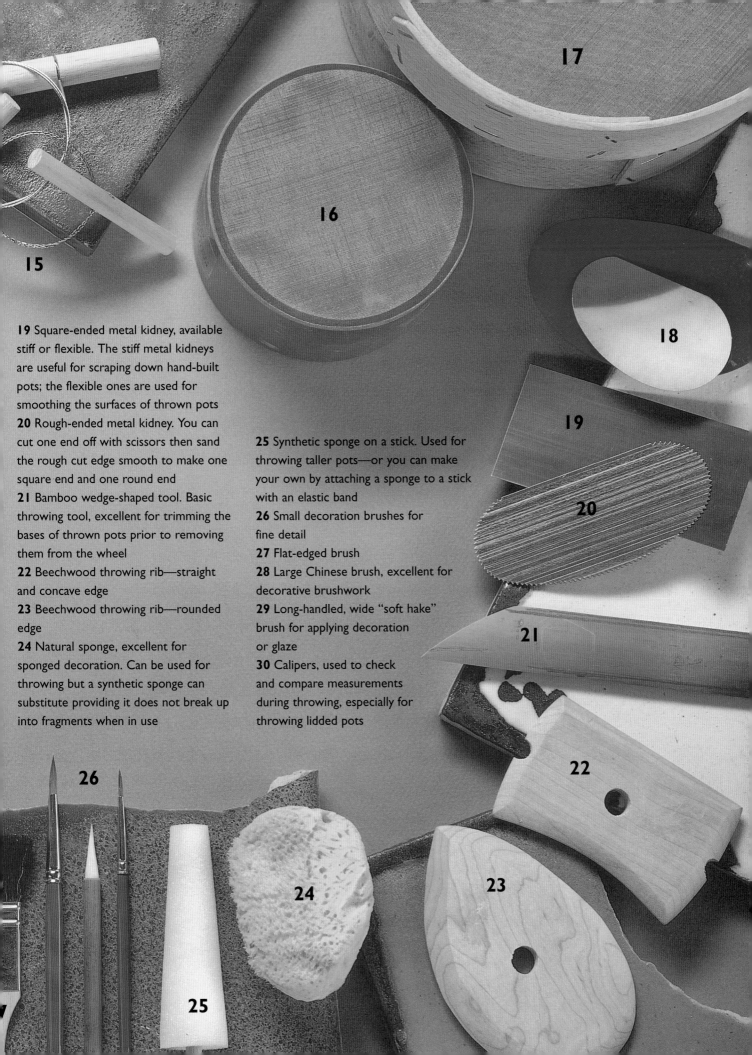

15

16

17

18

19

20

21

22

23

24

25

26

19 Square-ended metal kidney, available stiff or flexible. The stiff metal kidneys are useful for scraping down hand-built pots; the flexible ones are used for smoothing the surfaces of thrown pots
20 Rough-ended metal kidney. You can cut one end off with scissors then sand the rough cut edge smooth to make one square end and one round end
21 Bamboo wedge-shaped tool. Basic throwing tool, excellent for trimming the bases of thrown pots prior to removing them from the wheel
22 Beechwood throwing rib—straight and concave edge
23 Beechwood throwing rib—rounded edge
24 Natural sponge, excellent for sponged decoration. Can be used for throwing but a synthetic sponge can substitute providing it does not break up into fragments when in use

25 Synthetic sponge on a stick. Used for throwing taller pots—or you can make your own by attaching a sponge to a stick with an elastic band
26 Small decoration brushes for fine detail
27 Flat-edged brush
28 Large Chinese brush, excellent for decorative brushwork
29 Long-handled, wide "soft hake" brush for applying decoration or glaze
30 Calipers, used to check and compare measurements during throwing, especially for throwing lidded pots

CLAY

John Leach *Thrown pot, fired inside a saggar (see Glossary) with sawdust.*

Pick up a piece of soft clay. What you have in your hand, at its most basic, is igneous rock particles, water, and millions of year of time.

Igneous rock is derived from magma or lava. These granites form most of the earth's crust, so clay is abundant worldwide. The transformation from rock to clay begins under the earth's surface before the magma or lava has cooled and become rigid. Hot gasses from within the earth decompose the rock, breaking it up into particles. The feldspar particles of the rock then decompose further to form what is known as primary clay.

The most commonly used primary clay is china clay, which is composed of alumina, silica and water. Most china clays have large, rough-shaped particles making the clay unworkable in its pure state, because it does not have the "plasticity" needed for making forms. It is, however, very useful as an addition to other clays, slips, or glazes and can be blended with other materials to make porcelain.

Most pottery making requires the clay to be "plastic," so the next phase in the decomposing of the primary clay is essential. The primary clays get washed away from their original site, often going

downstream in rivers of water or ice. This action grinds down the rough edges of the clay particles, and these smaller, smoother particles can also become mixed with other materials such as iron oxide and vegetable matter. The clay which is found away from the original igneous rock site is known as secondary clay, and it is this which potters use.

There are many different types of secondary clay, all with individual qualities. They are found in layered seams at different depths, and the seams can vary considerably, so most potters use commercially prepared clays which have been carefully blended from different seams to give more consistent results.

Two main types of secondary clay are:

Earthenware clays, usually fired between 1970°–2100°F (1080° to 1150°C). These remain porous even after firing. Earthenware clays contain minerals which would melt at higher temperatures, making the shapes bloat and distort. Earthenware clay can be white to brown in color depending on the iron oxide content.

Stoneware clays, usually fired to between 2190–2460°F (1200 to 1350°C). Stoneware clays do not have the large amounts of the fluxes found in earthenware, so they can be fired up to the point where the clay softens. This allows the clay to fuse and integrate more strongly with the glaze layer and makes the unglazed clay relatively vitreous (glass-like).

CLAY PARTICLE ALIGNMENT

Clay is made up from flat, hexagonal-shaped particles. In newly mixed, wet clay, these plate-like particles will be placed randomly with each other rather

than in flat parallel alignment. This can make the soft clay less stretchable and prone to having fine crack lines on the surface when it is bent into a round shape (known as "short" clay). When the clay particles are randomly placed there is more water space in between them, causing the clay to shrink slightly more when drying.

Kneading and then storing freshly made, soft clay for eight to ten weeks in an airtight container will help to remedy this, because the pressure flattens the particles against each other to form parallel layers, thus making the clay more stretchable, or "plastic." The water layer in between the flat particles allows them to slide over each other, but also holds them together with suction, just as water in between two sheets of glass will hold them together but allow sliding movement. It is this ability of the flat clay particles to slide over each other which enables wet clay to be stretched and formed into any shape desired.

TENSIONING THE CLAY

When making clay forms it is important to apply equal pressure to all surfaces to ensure that the clay particles are aligned equally. This will allow for more even drying. It is particularly important to apply pressure on the bases of pots because they don't otherwise get pressed as much as the walls during making. For example, the base of the coil-built vase on pages 42–43 and the bases of all of the thrown pots have been given an extra pressing down process, which is known as tensioning. Without this, the bases of these pots would be more likely to dry with an S-shaped crack because the non-aligned clay in the base will shrink more than the compressed aligned clay in the walls of the pot.

RECLAIMING AND PREPARING CLAY

Very little clay need ever be wasted, because any unfired clay can be soaked in water and reclaimed to be used over and over again. Begin by putting any scraps of dry clay into a bucket or other watertight container. Break up any large lumps of dry clay, and allow them to soak until there are no hard lumps (the amount of time needed will depend on the size of the dry clay pieces). Cover your reclaim bins to prevent anything from falling in and contaminating your clay; it is important to ensure that the clay has nothing else mixed into it except water. Remove the top layer of water using a jug or sponge.

Now follow these steps to return the clay scraps into clay ready for use.

1 Drying the clay scraps
Scoop a layer of scraps approximately 2 in. (5 cm.) thick onto a dry plaster bat. Ensure that there are no hard lumps of clay within the scraps. Newly thrown pots of soft clay that have collapsed while throwing on the wheel can be put straight onto the plaster bat to dry before reclaiming.

2 When clay has dried sufficiently to peel the dry side up from the bat, turn it over to dry the other side, then pick it up and push it into a solid lump. Take care to not let the clay dry too much, because the wedging and kneading processes will also dry it out. You need the clay to be as soft as possible.

3 Wedging the clay
Cut the lump in half with a cutting wire, then pick up the top half and throw it down onto the bottom half. Turn the lump over on its side, cut through the middle, pick up the top half and again bang it down onto the bottom piece.

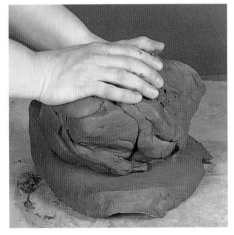

4 Continue to cut, turn, and slam the soft clay together in this pattern until it is homogeneous, with no soft or hard areas. As you slam the clay together, avoid trapping air in the clay by keeping the surface smooth with no air gaps.

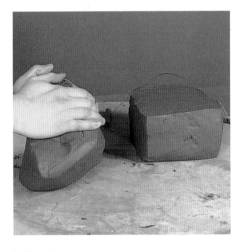

5 Kneading the clay
Kneading clay requires practice and patience. Kneading is like throwing in that it is done with a continuous movement which is difficult to explain, but here are some basic pointers to help you to get started. Begin with a reasonable sized lump of soft, wedged clay—a 5 lb. (2.25 kg.) lump is shown here—and put your hands on either side with your fingers wrapped round towards the back.

6 Stand with one foot in front of the other, lean your body forward onto your front foot as you press the palms of both hands with equal force into the clay lump. Take care to press the clay away from you rather than straight down (as pressing down will only flatten the clay). The clay should form a curved base.

7 Now lean back with the weight on your back leg—as you tip the lump up and towards you, lightly lifting it with your fingers. Now repeat steps 5 and 6 and continue kneading the clay until it is completely free of any trapped air.

8 Here, one hand has been removed to give a better view of the shape of the kneaded clay. The deep hollow is where the palm of the right hand pushed into the clay. This is at the end of pushing the clay forward. Note the curve of the base of the clay lump. This method of kneading is called the "ox face" or "bear face" because it resembles an animal's head. Note also the spiralling layers of clay made from the repeated kneading action.

9 The process of kneading spirals the clay around and around so that the solid lump has been turned inside out and back again. This process helps to put the clay particles into an even alignment, and also ensures that any trapped air bubbles will eventually be pushed out to the surface where they will be pressed against the bench and burst. It takes much kneading to ensure your clay is air-free. To check for air bubbles, use a cutting wire to slice through the lump. Slice through repeated layers to check the entire lump of clay, pressing the layers carefully back together afterwards to avoid trapping further air. It is especially important to have homogeneous, air-free clay for wheel-thrown pots, because any air bubbles will create a bulge, making it more difficult to keep on center.

10 For this photograph, red and white earthenware have been kneaded only three turns round and sliced in half to illustrate the spiralling process. If you have two different colored clays, you can either knead them together until completely blended, or use them as marbled clay for press-molding or throwing. This clay was used to throw the two mugs shown on page 109. Take care to test fire the mixed clays first, as they may not shrink at the same rates.

Spiral kneading

Another way of kneading clay, which is especially useful for larger lumps, is known as spiral kneading. The bulk of the clay spirals around the outside rim of the lump while your hands knead only a portion at a time. With this method, one hand does most of the pushing down, rather than the two hands pushing evenly. Begin with your hands at the top of the soft lump of clay, then push down using pressure from one hand and on only the top handful of clay on the lump. Lift the lump up with your other hand and twist it around slightly, repeating this action as the clay spirals. This is a difficult process to learn, so it is recommended that you seek out a potter who can teach you.

THE MAXIMUM THICKNESS OF CLAY

It is important to realize that no clay can make solid shapes of more than about ¾ in. (2 cm.) thick without having problems in the firing. This is because there are gases emitted from the clay which must be released through the surface of the pot during firing. However, the outside of a thick piece of clay will be heated up before the inner clay and, as the outside surface reaches the temperature where the pores shrink and close up, this seals the surface, trapping in the steam and other gases still being produced by the inner clay. This trapped steam builds up enough pressure to "blow out" the clay form, creating chunks of broken clay.

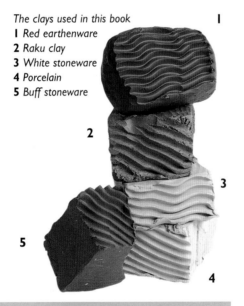

The clays used in this book
1 *Red earthenware*
2 *Raku clay*
3 *White stoneware*
4 *Porcelain*
5 *Buff stoneware*

THE CLAYS USED FOR THE PROJECTS

Different clays will have different firing temperatures for both bisque (biscuit) firing and glaze firing, so take care to check the correct firing temperatures with your supplier.

Red earthenware Bisque (biscuit) fired to 1830°F (1000°C); glaze fired to 2050°F (1120°C).

A high-firing red earthenware has been chosen for its rich coloring and to make the tablewares more chip resistant.

Raku Bisque (biscuit) fired to 1830°F (1000°C); top temperature 2370°F (1300°C) but has good strength at much lower temperatures.

Raku clay has a high percentage of coarse grog which helps it to withstand thermal shock.

Buff stoneware Bisque (biscuit) fired to 1830°F (1000°C); top firing temperature 2330°F (1280°C).

A lightly grogged clay which is suitable for both hand modeling and throwing. Unfired stoneware clay may be gray or even black from vegetable matter which burns out in the firing. The fired color of stoneware clay depends upon its iron oxide content and usually fires a buff-beige color in an electric kiln.

White stoneware clay Bisque (biscuit) fires to 2010°F (1100°C); top firing temperature 2330°F (1280°C).

A clay with virtually no iron oxide content and so fires to a creamy white color.

Porcelain Bisque (biscuit) fires to 2010°F (1100°C); top firing temperature 2370°F (1300°C).

Porcelain will be translucent if potted thinly and fired to its maturing temperature. It is made from china clay (a primary clay which is usually too coarse to make a "plastic" clay). Most procelains are blends of china clay with other materials.

CLAY STORAGE

Store wet clay in airtight containers. Many potters keep these in old refrigerators or freezers, but be sure the doors can be opened from the inside or there could be a danger of children getting trapped inside and suffocating.

Ready-made clay bought from suppliers will be delivered in plastic bags. Even though this clay should be soft and without air bubbles, it still requires the kneading process to align the clay particles and ensure the clay softness is homogeneous. Remove clay with a cutting wire rather than your hands to avoid trapping air in the clay, then reseal the bag at the top to prevent clay stuck to the sides of the bag from drying and then attaching to the soft clay. Soft clay must always be kept sealed in an airtight container, as even a short time left uncovered will dry the clay.

SLIP

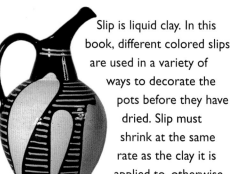

Molly Curly
Dipped, poured, and trailed slip.

Slip is liquid clay. In this book, different colored slips are used in a variety of ways to decorate the pots before they have dried. Slip must shrink at the same rate as the clay it is applied to, otherwise it is likely to crack during drying or firing. The simplest way to ensure that your slip and clay will shrink at the same rate is to use the same clay used for the body, made into liquid form, as the base slip. Ask your supplier if the clay can be bought in powder form, as it is much quicker to mix a slip from powder than from solid wet clay.

If, however, the clay you are using is darker than the slip you would like, you can make a white base slip from powdered clays. One possibility is to mix half china clay to half ball clay, but test fire this to see if it shrinks at the same rate as your own clay.

ADDING COLORANTS TO SLIP

To make your own colored slips you can add up to 5% of metal oxides, or up to 15% of commercial colorants (approximately double the amount needed to color glazes). The percentage of metal oxide or commercial colorant needed to achieve the desired color will depend on the base slip, the glaze used, and the firing temperature, so it is essential to make and fire tests to achieve good results. The colored slips in this book were made by adding 10% commercial colorant to the white stoneware clay used for the projects. It was mixed in powder form with water and sieved (see pp.16–19). You can buy ready-made slips in handy, lidded containers.

Blue, green, and yellow slip.

WHEN TO APPLY SLIP

It is vital to apply slip to the wares before the clay pot has dried past the leatherhard stage. Because slip is liquid clay, it must dry and shrink along with the clay it is applied to. If slip is applied to a dry pot, it is more likely to crack as it dries and shrinks because the dry pot will already have shrunk.

SLIP THICKNESS

It is also important to have the slip made up to the correct thickness for the decoration. Slip should be the consistency of light cream for pouring and dipping pots into, and thicker (more like heavy cream) for slip trailing. If slip is applied too thinly the clay underneath will show through, but if it is applied too thickly it is more likely to crack. The best way to learn the correct thickness for the different types of application is to make tests first.

Just as with glaze, a slip should be made the day before it is required so that it will settle overnight and the excess water separated on top can be removed. This top layer of water should always be removed before stirring slips, as the water can then be added back to the slip or glaze to make it just the right thickness.

Slips will settle to the bottom of the containers, so it is important to stir them repeatedly during use and to shake slip trailers to mix the slip.

SLIP TRAILING

Slip trailers should be kept full, to prevent trapped air from spluttering slip out unexpectedly when slip trailing.

For trailing, the slip needs to be thick enough not to run, but thin enough not to clog the nozzle; it should also be well sieved to ensure there are no lumps. There are different types of slip trailer available from ceramic suppliers, some with thin, hard, plastic nozzles and others made of soft rubber.

STORING SLIP

Slips need to be stored in lidded airtight containers, otherwise the water content will evaporate, creating a thick skin on top. The insides of the containers should be wiped clean after use to prevent the splashes of slip on the container walls from drying and falling into the slip, making it lumpy.

THE MAIN DRYING STAGES OF CLAY

Water can make up a third of the weight of soft clay. Water lubricates the clay particles enabling them to slide over each other to make the clay stretch (giving the clay "plastic" qualities). As clay dries, most of the water evaporates from the clay making it shrink (the amount of shrinkage is different for different clays but tends to be from 5% to 8% in the size of the pot). Completely dry clay still contains water however. This water is chemically bound up in the clay and is released during the firing process, making the clay shrink yet again. So most prepared clays will shrink in size by approximately 10% from soft to fired. Wet clay contains water in three main areas. There is chemically bound water within the clay which is not released until the firing process. Then there is water forming a thin film that surrounds each flat clay particle ("lubricating" the clay), with most of the water content filling the gaps in between these clay particles.

THE LEATHERHARD STAGE OF DRYING

When wet clay is exposed to air, the water will start to evaporate from the surface of the clay. The remaining water in the clay migrates through the gaps in between the clay particles to evaporate. This migration of water pulls the thin film of water away from the individual clay particles until they are touching each other and can therefore no longer slide over each others' surface. At this point there is still water filling the gaps in between the dry clay particles. This is called the leatherhard stage—sometimes also referred to as "cheese hard."

DRY WORK EVENLY

Care must be taken to ensure that clay forms dry evenly, otherwise the stress caused by one part of a form drying before the rest can cause the shape to distort and crack.

If at all possible, the work should be turned upside-down to expose the base for drying. For example, thrown pots should be twisted and lifted off the work board as soon as they are dry enough to do this without distorting their shape. The work board should then be sponged

Airtight, lidded containers can store small unfinished pots for a few days.

clean, a large sheet of plastic placed on it, and the pots placed upside-down on top. This will prevent the rims of the pots from drying further. Garbage bin bags cut open or the plastic that dry cleaners wrap clothes in are useful for this.

PREVENTING UNFINISHED WORK FROM DRYING FURTHER

If you have not finished the pots, enclose them in plastic sheeting so that no air

can get to them. They can then be finished the next day. If pots are placed onto dry, absorbent surfaces such as wooden boards rather than plastic sheeting, the wooden surface will absorb water from the pots and dry them.

Unfinished work can also be prevented from drying further by placing it in a lidded, airtight container such as those used for food storage. Larger work can be sealed in large plastic bags, though beware that some plastic can actually "breathe" and thus allow the clay to dry.

FINAL DRYING

When clay dries beyond the leatherhard stage the surface will turn a lighter color, first on exposed edges and then all over. The water is evaporating from within the gaps between the clay particles, making the clay very brittle. Generally, any joins made on clay which has even slightly passed the leatherhard stage will be prone to cracking.

Drying finished pots should be done slowly and evenly. Plastic sheeting draped over the top of work, or over exposed thin areas of a form can even out the drying, as can covering the entire form with dry sheets of newspaper, which prevents drafts (draughts) from affecting the drying.

When the clay is completely dry it will no longer feel cool to touch—by putting your cheek to the work you will be able to feel any moisture in the clay as a coolness on the surface. The length of time it takes to dry a piece completely will depend on the type of clay used, how thick the piece is, and the heat and humidity of the room.

When the clay is completely dry it is ready to be bisque (biscuit) fired.

Monika Debus
Hand-thrown tableware, decorated with colored slips and finished with a transparent glaze.

GLAZE

Underglaze colors in pencil-form.

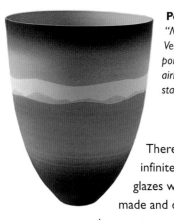

Peter Lane
"Mountain Skies Vessel," thrown porcelain, airbrushed ceramic stains, unglazed.

There are an infinite variety of glazes which can be made and developed to give a vast range of color, texture, and pattern, but this book deals only with the use of ready-made glazes—making them, applying them to your work, and adding coloring oxides or colorants to them. A wide range of reliable, ready-made glazes is available from ceramic suppliers. Three of these were purchased for the projects: a transparent earthenware glaze which has a firing range between 1940–2120°F (1060 to 1160°C); a transparent stoneware glaze with a firing range of between 2260–2370°F (1240 to 1300°C) and for the project on page 42, a very low-temperature "raku" glaze (see Glossary) which fires to 1740°F (950°C). They were used both as transparent glazes and as the "base" glazes to which other minerals were added to give color or opaqueness. All were fired in an electric kiln and are therefore oxidized.

WHAT IS GLAZE?

Glaze is glass made from silica (the main ingredient), alumina (needed to stiffen the glass and prevent it from running off the sides of pots during the firing); and flux (needed to lower the melting point of the silica).

Silica, alumina, and flux are found in many different rock minerals which are made into finely grained powders. For example, the same igneous rock which

decomposes to make clay also yields feldspars which are common stoneware glaze ingredients. These ground powders are mixed in proportions which will melt at the desired temperature for the clay used. Other materials can be added to affect the color or texture of the glaze or to make it more opaque.

The practical purpose of glaze, which has been used for thousands of years, is to turn a porous clay surface into a non-porous one. It is thus important for making tablewares more hygienic for food and drink (see health warning on p.18). Surfaces not intended for food or drink can be left unglazed and still fired to the maturing temperature of the clay to show the qualities of the clay itself.

UNDERGLAZE COLORS

Underglaze colors can be bought in a variety of forms including powdered, as chalks or pencils, or in tubes ready to be mixed with water. They can be applied to soft or leatherhard clay and to bisque (biscuit) fired ware. Some of the colors can be mixed but, as with all ceramic colors, should be test fired first, as the metal oxides which they are made of make them less predictable than paint colors. Many underglaze colors can be fired up to 2370°F (1300°C) without burning out in the firing, so underglaze decoration can be applied both to earthenware and stoneware clay.

Underglaze must not be applied in too thick a layer or the glaze will bubble in the firing. Adding a small amount of liquid gum arabic to the underglaze will

help to prevent it from smudging when handling the pot (see toxic hazard warning on page 18).

OVERGLAZE ENAMELS

Overglaze enamels are colors which flux at much lower temperatures than glazes. Those used in this book, applied to the finished glossy glaze surface of the butter dish on pages 70–72, were fired to 1430°F (780°C). They are usually applied to finished glaze-fired wares. The texture of the fired enamels will be affected by the glaze on the pot; if it is shiny the enamels will be glossy and bright, but if the surface is unglazed or has a matte finish the fired enamels will be dry and duller in color.

You can buy ready-made finished pots or tiles, known as "blank ware," to decorate, but these should first be put in a kiln and fired to 1830°F (1000°C) to drive out any moisture which may be trapped inside. Otherwise the enamel firing may leave the glazed surface pitted and spoiled.

Enamels can be water- or oil-based. The blue and yellow enamels used in this book are water-based so they are thinned with just water, and brushes can be cleaned in the same way. The gold luster is oil-based, so special thinners must be used. Ask your supplier for advice about this. Both the colored enamels and the gold luster were fired to 1430°F (780°C) (see toxic hazard

Underglaze powders mixed with water.

MIXING GLAZE WITH METAL OXIDES OR COLORANTS

Different glazes will have different color responses when mixed with colorants and fired. The thickness of the glaze also affects the color, as does the clay used and the different types of kiln firing (see p.22). The only way to learn what colors and surfaces will look like is to make and fire glaze tests of varying thicknesses on the clay you intend to use—which has been bisque (biscuit) fired to the same temperature as the non-test pieces. But it is remarkable that even after making extensive tests, most makers are still never exactly sure how a glaze will turn out on their finished work until it is safely out of the glaze firing, which can be both exhilarating and frustrating. If colored slips or underglaze colors are used, glazes must also, of course, be tested on these.

In general you can base your first glaze color tests on the following:

COMMERCIALLY PREPARED GLAZE COLORANTS

Additions of 2% to 10% should yield colors ranging from very light through to bold. Beware that adding much more than 10% can cause the glaze to bubble.

Iron oxide: 1% to 10% will tend to yield colors from cream to beige to brown and black in an electric kiln.

Copper oxide: ½% to 3% will tend to give turquoise blue in alkaline earthenware glazes and green in other glazes fired in an electric kiln.

Cobalt oxide: ¼% to 2% will tend to give light to navy blue coloring.

Rutile (a titanium ore which contains iron oxide): 5% to 15% will tend to yield opaque oatmeal, mustard yellow to brown mottled surfaces in an electric kiln.

Tin oxide: up to 10% will tend to make glazes opaque and white. Commercially

prepared colorants and oxides can be combined in the same glazes to give interesting results, but do not add too much colorant as this can make the glaze run onto your kiln shelves during the firing, or it can produce dry, black, cratered surfaces.

TIP

Make bisque (biscuit) fired clay slabs and fire your glaze tests on top of them so that if any glazes run during the firing they will drip onto the slab and not spoil your kiln shelves.

HOW TO MIX GLAZE

Ready-made glazes can be bought in a wide range of colors and textures from ceramic material suppliers. They can be bought mixed with water, or as dry powders. If your glaze arrives in powder form then follow Steps 2 and 5 to prepare it. You can also add coloring materials to the ready-made glazes as follows.

After preparing the glaze, use an indelible pen to make a label to attach to the container, noting the glaze ingredients and firing temperature. Most liquid glazes look alike and you can quickly forget what containers hold what. A fired test piece is also useful to attach to the container as a reference. Always make clear notes of your glaze tests. Many potters keep a glaze book in which they record all of the glazes and variations they have tried. This is especially helpful if you also write down the results of the glaze tests for future reference.

EQUIPMENT

Face mask with appropriate dust filters

Rubber gloves

Accurate weighing scales

Plastic containers for mixing

Lidded plastic containers for glaze storage

80 mesh sieve for slips

120 mesh sieve for glazes

TOOLS

Stiff brush to stir the liquid through the sieve

Sticks to support the sieve over the container

Adhesive labels and an indelible pen to label all containers

MATERIALS

Leatherhard test pieces to test slips on

Bisque (biscuit) fired test pieces to test glazes on

Ready-made glaze powder

Commercially prepared glaze colorants or metal oxides

1 Mixing in coloring materials
A ready-made transparent glaze powder can be mixed with metal oxides and/or commercially prepared colorants to give color. Use a face mask with a dust filter and wear rubber gloves. Carefully weigh an amount of the glaze powder. 3½ oz. (100g.) is being weighed out here.

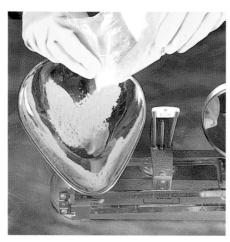

2 The glaze powder is now added to approximately 1 cup (250 ml.) of ordinary tap water. If the water is poured into the glaze it is more likely to make it lumpy. More water is used than required for the thickness of the glaze because it will help to mix the glaze and allow it to pass through the sieve more easily.

3 To make the glaze yellow, 10% of commercially prepared yellow glaze colorant is added. 10% of the 3½ oz. (100 g.) of transparent glaze (weighed out in step 1) would weigh ⅜ oz. (10 g.), so this amount of the yellow colorant is weighed. It is added to the wet glaze mixture and they are stirred together.

4 Sieving the glaze
The yellow glaze mixture must now be sieved through a 120 mesh sieve to ensure that all of the ingredients are thoroughly mixed together and that there are no gritty materials that need to be removed. Ordinary kitchen sieves are not fine enough; you will need to buy the sieve or its mesh from ceramic suppliers. Larger amounts of glaze will require larger sieves.

WARNING

Dust hazard
All clay or glaze dust is harmful if inhaled, so when using clay and glaze powders you must always wear an adequate protective face mask with appropriate dust filters (available where ceramic supplies are sold). Always use wet sponges to clean surfaces after use, and use vacuum cleaners or wet mops, rather than sweeping with brooms or brushes.

Toxic hazard
Many raw glaze ingredients (including the metal oxides and carbonates, the commercially prepared underglaze colorants used for coloring and opacity, and the overglaze enamel colors) are also toxic if ingested, so it is safest to treat all unfired glaze ingredients as toxic unless you are certain they are not. Do not inhale or ingest even small amounts of these materials.
Some glaze ingredients can be absorbed through skin. Some, like the alkaline ingredients, can be an irritant to skin. It is therefore important to wear protective rubber gloves when handling glaze materials and not to get any in your eyes.
Always keep all glaze materials safely out of reach of children.
Ask your supplier for safety information on the materials you buy.

Surfaces intended for food and drink
There are also some glaze ingredients which are not only toxic in their raw, unfired state, but can remain soluble and therefore toxic in some glazes even after the glaze firing, making the glazed surface unsafe for food or drink. Check labels of all glazes for food-safe information. For example, one common ingredient of earthenware glazes is lead "frit" (see Glossary). This can be made into safe glazes which pass the food standard health and safety tests for lead release. However, if glazes containing lead frit have been made or fired incorrectly, or have certain substances like copper added, then the glaze would not be safe for food or drink as the lead in the glaze will be more soluble.
In addition to lead products, there are other minerals which may be soluble even in a fired glaze, thereby making the glaze unsafe for food or drink.
The main materials to avoid are lead, barium, cadmium, lithium, strontium, and zinc.

Overglaze enamels
Although the overglaze enamels shown in the butter-dish project on pages 70–72 are lead-free, they still should not be used on any surface which is intended for food or drink. This is because the enamels are only fired to 1430°F (780°C), which is too low a temperature for them to melt into and make a strong bond with the glaze layer. Enamels can therefore be scraped off the surface of the glaze relatively easily, making them unsuitable for food or drink surfaces (unless advised otherwise by your suppliers). It is safe to decorate the outside of a container, as shown with the butter dish.

Selecting your glaze and decoration materials
The ready-made glazes, the underglaze colors, and the overglaze enamels used in this book are lead-, barium-, lithium-, strontium-, zinc-, and cadmium-free. These glazes and colors give food finished results without the added risk of containing the potentially soluble and toxic materials. You can ask your supplier for materials which do not contain lead, barium, lithium, strontium, zinc, or cadmium when selecting ready-made glazes, underglaze colors, and overglaze enamels.
If you have any doubt about using or firing any glaze material or coloring material, you must seek further advice to ensure safety.

Note: All of the five steps can be adapted for mixing slips. The only difference is that you will use an 80 mesh sieve and mix the slips thicker than glaze, about the consistency of light cream, or heavy for slip trailing.

If the glaze has settled to a hard lump which is difficult to stir, then a few drops of calcium chloride solution will help to keep it in suspension and prevent it from setting so solid. If this continues to be a problem, a teaspoon of "bentonite" powder can be added to the dry glaze powder before both are put in water. The bentonite and calcium chloride work together to prevent the glaze from setting solid. Bentonite must be mixed well into dry glaze powder before being added to water or it becomes a slimy mess.

After glazing, wipe clean the insides of the glaze container before putting its lid on. This will prevent splashes of glaze drying on the sides of the container and dropping down into the glaze, forming small hard lumps.

5 Making glaze tests

After mixing glazes they must be left to settle for 24 hours. The heavier glaze particles will settle to the bottom, leaving a layer of water on top. Carefully pour off this water, or use a jug or sponge to remove it, but do not discard the liquid. Now put on rubber gloves and stir the glaze with your hand, feeling to ensure there are no lumps. Add back some of the water until the glaze is the desired thickness (generally just thicker than milk for transparent glaze and the thickness of light cream for stoneware glazes). When the glaze is well stirred, it is ready to have bisque (biscuit) fired test pieces dipped in for two seconds, then pulled out and held over the container to drain. When the sheen has dried off the surface, part of the test piece should again be dipped into the glaze and removed. Repeat this to give an idea of what the glaze is like if applied thin, medium, or thick. Now carefully wipe off all of the glaze from the bottom edge of the test pieces and glaze fire them on top of a bisque (biscuit) fired slab of clay to protect your shelves from any drips or runny glaze. Glaze can also be applied by brushing on layers of glaze with a brush.

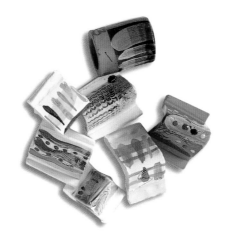

Assorted glaze test pieces.

MAKING TEST PIECES

The test pieces should be made with any colored slips or underglaze colors applied on them which you intend to use on your finished pieces, so that you will see how the glaze reacts with them. Test pieces should not necessarily be flat tiles. Glazes intended for vertical surfaces should be tested on vertical surfaces, as some can be prone to running. These test pieces were made by shaping leatherhard slabs of clay into A shapes. They have deep score marks on the surface to show how the glaze behaves on sharp edges and in deep hollows. A hole has been cut through the back which would enable the test piece to be strung together with others, mounted on a wall panel or attached to the container of glaze as a reference to how the glaze fires. Test pieces can also be made in the shape of small hollow tubes, which again are convenient for stringing together.

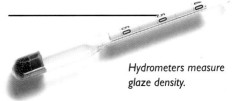

Hydrometers measure glaze density.

CALCULATING THE DRY WEIGHT OF A LIQUID GLAZE OR SLIP

If you begin with liquid slip or glaze rather than the dry powder, you will need to calculate the dry weight, because the percentages given for colorings are intended for dry, not wet, weights. To do this, put a measured amount of the well-stirred slip or glaze into a container and weigh this. Now fill the same (or an identical) container with water to the same level and weigh this. The container full of slip or glaze will weigh more than the container of water. By subtracting the weight of the container of water from the weight of the container of slip or glaze, you will then have the dry weight, and will be able to calculate percentages.

For example if a cup of liquid slip weighs 9 oz. (260 g.), and the same cup filled to the same level with water weighs 5 oz. (140 g.), then the dry weight of the slip will be 4 oz. (120 g.). Ten percent of this would be ½ oz. (12 g.), five percent would be .2 oz. (6 g.) etc.

PLASTER

Steve Mattison
"Sky Series," press-molded colored clay, raku fired.

Working with plaster can be a messy business, but it is essential that absolutely *no* plaster ever contaminates your clay or glaze. It is therefore vital that all surfaces are thoroughly cleaned after mold making, especially if you use the same space for clay work. Clay used for mold making should be kept in a separate lidded airtight container, and can be re-used for other plaster work, but never to make pots with. Even small amounts of plaster can spoil your pottery because the plaster "blows out" of the clay during the firing, creating a pitted hole in the surface of the pot.

Plaster will also clog drains so everything should be washed in a large container of water, not in the sink (an old baby bath is ideal for this). The water should be left to settle, then the clean water on top can be safely poured down the sink (it could be run through a large mesh sieve first to ensure no lumps go down the sink). Then the plaster which has settled at the bottom can be scooped out and thrown away. Plaster, unlike clay, cannot be re-used once it has set.

Plaster sets within minutes of being added to water, so it is vital to have everything well prepared in advance of the mixing. It is better to pour a mold with one batch of plaster. However, if your mold turns out to need more plaster than you have mixed, score the top in a crosshatch pattern using a sharp pointed tool, then mix and pour more plaster onto this to complete the mold. This must be done within a few hours of the original plaster mix to ensure a strong bond between the two mixes.

When the plaster begins to set, a chemical reaction takes place which causes it to heat up. Placing your hand on the mold, you will feel it warm up within moments of going hard. Only when it has cooled down again is it strong enough to have the walls removed around the mold and the rough edges of the plaster scraped down.

1 Mixing plaster

Use cold water, as warm water will make the plaster set much more quickly. Measure the correct amount of water needed for the mold. The plaster used for these projects requires 1 pint (575 ml.) of water to 1 lb. 13 oz. (775 g.) of plaster. If more water is added, the set plaster will be more porous and absorbent but also much softer and easily broken. With less water, the plaster will set harder but will be much less absorbent.

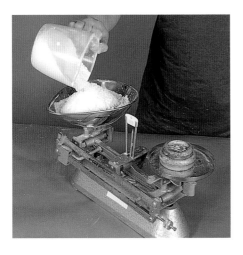

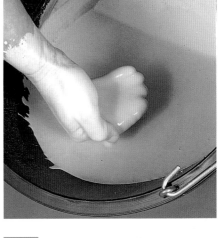

2 Weigh the correct amount of plaster for the mold. Plaster should always be bought fresh and stored in an airtight, lidded container or plastic bag because plaster absorbs moisture from the atmosphere. This added moisture makes old plaster lumpy to mix, and it will set in much less time—possibly a matter of a few seconds after the water has been added.

3 Sprinkle the plaster into the water fairly quickly, but avoid putting in big handfuls as this could create lumps. Sieving the plaster first, using an ordinary kitchen sieve (which should *never* be returned to the kitchen for food use), will help it to enter the water as individual particles and prevent lumps from forming.

6 Now the container holding the plaster should be gently agitated in order to encourage any air bubbles to rise to the surface. This action will form a froth which should be skimmed off the top and thrown away. Stretching a garbage bag over a cardboard box in advance will make it easier when you are working quickly with the setting plaster. As soon as the plaster changes from the thinness of milk to the thickness of cream, it is ready to pour into your prepared mold. Any excess plaster should be scooped into the bin, and then the container the plaster was mixed in should be thoroughly cleaned out (but not in the sink). It is very important to remove all traces of plaster from the container because even small amounts of dry plaster left in it will make the next batch of plaster set *much* more quickly and possibly leave you no time to pour it into the mold.

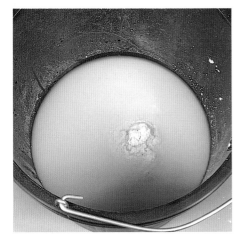

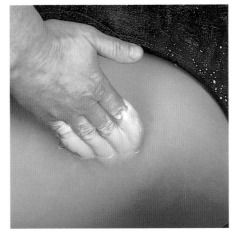

4 Leave the plaster to stand for one minute. This time allows the plaster to absorb the water evenly. If you begin mixing too soon, dry pockets of plaster in the mix will form lumps.

5 Now slide one hand down into the plaster mix to the bottom of the bucket. With your arm remaining as still as possible, move your fingers around to mix the plaster and water thoroughly and break up any lumps. The less your arm moves and agitates the surface, the fewer air bubbles will be added to the mix. This stirring should only take a few moments.

KILNS AND FIRING

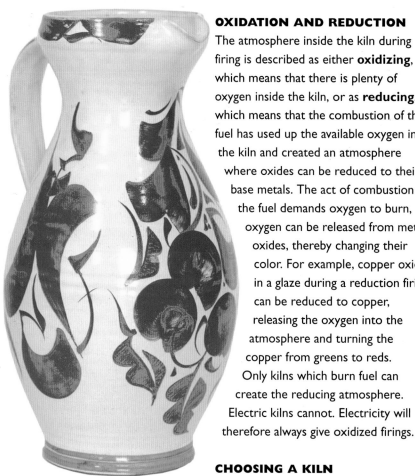

Alan Caiger-Smith
Jug with copper luster reduction.

There is a wide variety of kilns available. Kilns can be fired with a number of different energy sources, including electricity, gas (natural gas or propane), oil (including old "sump" oil from cars), wood, and coal.

There are many different firing controls on kilns, so you will need to get instructions on how to fire it from the manufacturer.

All kilns should have kiln shelves laid on the inside floor where the first layer of pots can be packed. This kiln shelf layer will protect the soft brick base of the kiln.

OXIDATION AND REDUCTION

The atmosphere inside the kiln during firing is described as either **oxidizing**, which means that there is plenty of oxygen inside the kiln, or as **reducing**, which means that the combustion of the fuel has used up the available oxygen in the kiln and created an atmosphere where oxides can be reduced to their base metals. The act of combustion of the fuel demands oxygen to burn, so oxygen can be released from metal oxides, thereby changing their color. For example, copper oxide in a glaze during a reduction firing can be reduced to copper, releasing the oxygen into the atmosphere and turning the copper from greens to reds. Only kilns which burn fuel can create the reducing atmosphere. Electric kilns cannot. Electricity will therefore always give oxidized firings.

CHOOSING A KILN

Electric kilns tend to be easier to fire than combustible fuel kilns, so they make good kilns for the beginner. They can be large enough to walk into or small enough for one person to pick up easily. One cubic foot sized kilns (i.e. 1 foot high by 1 foot wide by 1 foot deep internal dimensions) have the added advantage of often only needing a 2 pin (13 amp supply) for its power supply. Larger kilns will sometimes require more than a normal domestic electricity supply and can therefore prove to be very expensive to install. Always have a qualified electrician install electric kilns.

You will find plenty of second-hand electric kilns by looking through the classified ads of ceramic magazines. Take care, however, as many old electric kilns have poor insulation and are made of heavy bricks which take much longer to heat up and therefore consume far more fuel than modern well-insulated kilns made from light bricks. The money saved by buying a very old kiln could quickly be lost through higher electricity charges. One other advantage of buying a new kiln for the novice potter is that you can get valuable information on how to fire it from the suppliers, and they can also ensure that it is installed safely.

There are two main types of electric kilns: those which have the door on the side, opening like refrigerator doors, and those that have the lids on top, opening like chest freezers. Both types will have a spy hole in the side and a hole in the top which have specially made bungs.

BISQUE (BISCUIT) FIRING

Also known as the "first firing," bisque (biscuit) firing is done by most potters. It makes the pots easier to handle during glazing and prevents technical problems which are more common with "raw glazing"—the term used for pots glazed while still leatherhard, and only once fired up to the glaze temperature. Bisque (biscuit) firing transforms the clay into ceramic which is porous. This porosity enables the pot to soak in the water content of glaze and leave a thin layer of the glaze powder on its surface.

Different clays need different bisque (biscuit) firing temperatures and so you will have to ask the supplier of your clay what the optimum firing temperature is. When loading bisque (biscuit) firings the pots (which must be completely dry) can be packed close together with their surfaces touching. Take care to ensure, however, that the pots and kiln shelves are at least 1¼ in. (3 cm.) away from the walls of the kiln and the electric elements.

GLAZE FIRING

Also known as "gloss firing" this takes the pottery up to the temperature in which the powdery surface of the glaze melts to form the non-porous glazed surface on the pots. The temperature of the glaze firing will depend upon what type of clay the pots are made from. Earthenware clays will have glaze firings ranging in temperature from 1970–2100°F (1080 to 1150°C); and stoneware clays have glaze firing ranging in temperature from 2190–2460°F (1200 to 1350°C).

When packing pots into the kiln for glaze firings, great care must be taken to ensure that the glazed surfaces of the pots do not touch each other or any part of the kiln, the melting glaze will stick them together. As with bisque (biscuit) firing, the pots should be at least 1¼ in. (3 cm.) away from the walls of the kiln and the electric elements.

HOW LONG DOES A FIRING TAKE?

Bisque (biscuit) firing begins with the spy hole in the kiln door and the hole in the top of the kiln being left open for gases to escape from the kiln during the first part of the firing. Large, thick pots should be fired slowly: for example, not rising more than 120°F (50°C) per hour until they reach 1290°F (700°C), a dull red heat. You should then put the bungs into both the door of the kiln and over the hole on top and put the kiln onto full power until it has reached the top temperature.

Normal bisque (biscuit) firings of thinner-walled pots can rise 210°F (100°C) per hour until the kiln reaches 1290°F (700°C), when the bungs should be put in, and the kiln can be put onto full power until it has reached temperature.

Glaze firing also begins with the spy hole in the door and the hole in the top of the kiln left open. As with bisque (biscuit) firing, they are closed after the kiln

John Pollex, *plate. Buff-colored earthenware, brushed and sponged-colored slips, transparent glaze.*

reaches 1290°F (700°C). If the pots have previously been bisque (biscuit) fired it is usually safe to glaze fire thinly made pots slightly more quickly, for example the kiln could rise by 260°F (125°C) per hour up to 1290°F (700°C), when it is safe to put the kiln onto full power until the top temperature is reached. Some glazes will benefit from holding the top temperature

PROBLEMS

If the pots have portions of them "blown off" during the firing, it is usually caused either by firing pots which are not yet completely dry, so that steam builds up in the clay and explodes the top layer off, or by trying to fire the kiln too quickly for the size of the pots. Another cause would be if the clay was simply too thick for firing.

of the glaze firing for a period of time, which is called "soaking the kiln" (usually 20 minutes to an hour), as this can prevent the surface of a glaze from being pitted into "pin holes." Beware of over firing the glaze, however, as this can make it run and possibly spoil both your pot and the kiln shelf.

COOLING DOWN TIME

Both bisque (biscuit) firing and glaze firings should be left to cool down to below 120°F (50°C) before they are opened and unpacked. At this low temperature the kiln will feel cool to touch, and the pots can be picked up with bare hands. If kilns are opened while they are too hot, you risk cracking your pots and damaging your kiln, so resist the temptation to see inside until it is safe!

KEEPING NOTES

Always write down the details of how you fired your kiln, noting how and when the controls were altered; the temperatures reached; the shape of the fired cones (see page 26); and the general results of the firing. This "kiln log" will be invaluable as a guide to successful firings.

crack the shelves, and even the smallest hairline crack will cause the kiln shelves to weaken and break during the firings. Every time you pack a kiln, check the shelves for any signs of cracking, and if you find any, break them in half. Do not discard these broken halves, however, as they can be very useful.

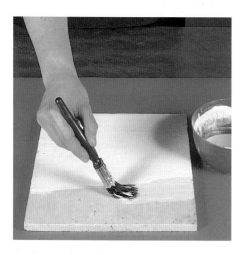

LOADING KILNS

To enable the space in the kiln to be filled, special shelves and props to hold up these shelves are used to stack up different layers in the kiln. The shelves and props are made from a highly refractory material called sillimanite, which will retain its form even at stoneware firing temperatures. To protect your kiln shelves you can paint a layer of kiln wash onto them. One commonly used recipe is to mix two parts of alumina with one part of china clay with water. A thin layer of this on kiln shelves will help to save the shelf if any glaze should drop onto it. The wash also prevents the clay bases of pots from becoming slightly fused to the shelf during the glaze firing. This is known as "plucking" and results in small portions of the clay breaking off of the base and adhering to the kiln shelf when the pot is removed after the firing.

Kiln shelves must be handled carefully because the material they are made from is very brittle. Rough handling can easily

Kiln props and stilts

Kiln props are available in a variety of heights. They can be stacked on top of each other to make the spaces in between the shelves just higher than the pots. They are made of the same material as the kiln shelves. Kiln shelves and props are referred to as "kiln furniture" and often are included with new kilns.

Stilts (shown on the right) are used to prop up the bases of pots from kiln shelves, enabling the entire base of the pot to be glazed. They tend not to be strong enough to withstand high-temperature firings, and so are normally

only used for low-temperature earthenware firings between 1970–2100°F (1080 to 1150°C). There are two main types of stilts. The three all-ceramic ones at the front should only be used once or until the points break off. The other stilts behind these are made of ceramic bases with special highly refractory metal points. These metal points make a much smaller mark on the base of the pot than the ceramic ones, and have the added advantage of being re-usable, so although they are initially more expensive to buy, they are more economical in the long run.

Stacking the kiln

Pots can be stacked rim to rim for the bisque (biscuit) firing, known as "boxing." This can be done in glaze firings, but only if the rims are completely unglazed, or the melted glaze will firmly stick them together. Selecting the prop height: it can be difficult to judge if the kiln props will be tall enough for the height of the pots, especially when using a top-loading kiln. If you set up two of the props on a table with a length of stick over the top, you will quickly see if they are the correct height. Here there is a clear gap between the top rim of the inverted bowl and the bottom edge of the stick.

Stacking tiles for firing

There are many specialty kiln props available. This tall stacking unit allows many industrially made tiles to be fired at once, saving much kiln space. Hand-made tiles can be stacked up using the individual metal-pointed stilts, though these will leave sharp points on the surface of the glaze which must be ground down after the firing.

WARNING

The extreme brightness of the heat in the kiln can damage your eyes, so protective welders' goggles should be worn when looking at the cones during the firing. The bung in the spy hole will become extremely hot during the firing, so you will need to wear an insulated protective glove when removing it to see the cones during firing. Also cones are toxic and must never be ingested—keep all pyrometric cones safely out of reach of children.

WARNING

See health and safety advice on page 7. Firing kilns can be hazardous. If you are ever in doubt, wait and seek further advice before firing your kiln.

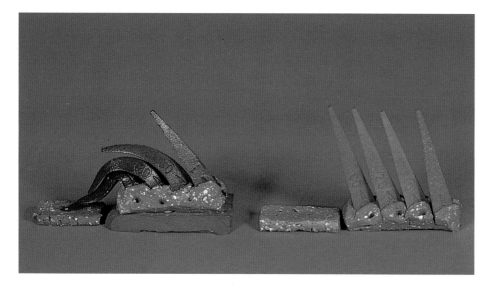

Pyrometric cones

The set of bent-over cones on the left have been fired to 2050°F (1120°C) with that temperature maintained ("soaking the kiln") for 20 minutes. The straight cones on the right have not yet been fired. A small piece of clay put in front of the cones will prevent the melted cone from sticking to the kiln itself.

Pyrometric cones are essential for ascertaining the effect of the heat on the pots inside the kiln during firing. The cones are set into soft clay at the slight angle that is cut on their base. They are then carefully placed inside the kiln just opposite the spy hole in the door of the kiln. (You may need to place a lighted candle inside the dark kiln when you are placing the cones to see them.) When the kiln is firing, the temperature makes the kiln glow inside, and the silhouettes of the cones will be visible when looking through the spy hole when the kiln is over 1290°F (700°C).

The cones are made from the same materials as glazes, and will melt at different temperatures, which is why they are numbered. It is advisable to use more than one cone for glaze firings. The first one to melt should be placed at the front of the row of cones. This is called the "guard" cone, because when it begins to bend over it indicates that the kiln is nearing the final temperature for firing.

Pyrometric cones

The set of bent-over cones on the left have been fired to 2050°F (1120°C) with that temperature maintained ("soaking the kiln") for 20 minutes. The straight cones on the right have not yet been fired. A small piece of clay put in front of the cones will prevent the melted cone from sticking to the kiln itself. Pyrometric cones are essential for ascertaining the effect of the heat on the pots inside the kiln during firing. The cones are set into soft clay at the slight angle that is cut on their base. They are then carefully placed inside the kiln just opposite the spy hole in the door of the kiln. (You may need to place a lighted candle inside the dark kiln when you are

---

TIP

Sometimes gritty dust can fall down from the roof of the kiln during firing, so it is a good idea to place a kiln shelf over the top of the final layer of pots to protect them from this. Kilns are made of very fragile materials which need careful treatment. It also helps to vacuum the inside of your kiln to remove unwanted grit or dust. The metal kiln elements especially should be vacuumed free of any clay or dust particles because if anything touches the metal element during firing it can cause that element to fuse, necessitating replacement.

Stacking the kiln

When stacking the kiln use three props to hold the shelves up—three will be more stable than four. It is very important to ensure that the props are placed one above the other throughout the stack of shelves as this will carry the weight of the shelves and pots directly down through the props. If the props are placed on one side for one shelf layer, then on another side for the next shelf layer, the weight from above will press down on the shelf, which can buckle and warp or even break under the pressure.

In the photograph there are two props in the left corners of the kiln and one prop in the middle of the right side. A kiln shelf can now be placed on top of these props. For the next layer, props again must be placed with two in the left corner and one prop in the middle of the right side.

BUILDING AND FIRING A SAWDUST KILN

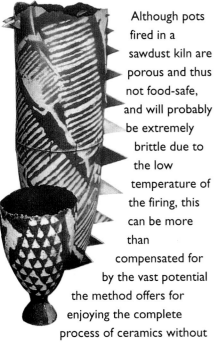

Although pots fired in a sawdust kiln are porous and thus not food-safe, and will probably be extremely brittle due to the low temperature of the firing, this can be more than compensated for by the vast potential the method offers for enjoying the complete process of ceramics without expensive equipment. Sawdust firing is also one of the best ways to achieve the rich, satiny jet-black surfaces on burnished ware.

The temperature your sawdust kiln reaches will be dependent upon many factors, including the size of the kiln, the weather, and the ventilation gaps on the lid. Larger sawdust kilns tend to achieve higher temperatures than small ones. At worst your kiln may only achieve a few hundred degrees fahrenheit. (This is insufficient to transform clay into ceramic and the pots will therefore need to be fired again.) A good firing could perhaps reach 1470°F (800°C).

If you do have access to a kiln capable of 1830°F (1000°C), then it is of course advisable to bisque (biscuit) fire the pots before sawdust firing, as this will cut down on the number of pieces broken in firing, and the finished pieces will be much less brittle—though still unsuitable for food or liquid.

left: **Meri Wells**
Coil-built "raku" fired vessels with black carbonized surfaces from sawdust smoking.

Always ensure that pots to be fired are completely dry. This can take days or weeks, depending on the temperature and humidity. If the pots are not going to be bisque (biscuit) fired first, it is a good precaution to prepare the already dry pot for sawdust firing by preheating it to approximately 140°F (60°C) for two hours in your kiln or in an ordinary kitchen oven. This preheating will drive out any remaining moisture in the clay, and it will also help to prevent thermal shock from cracking the pot during the sawdust firing. You will need to wear heat-resistant gloves to remove the pre-heated pot from the kiln or oven and place it in the prepared sawdust kiln.

MATERIALS

50 clay house bricks and a large kiln shelf or metal container

Metal lid

Sawdust

Wood shavings

Newspaper

Matches

EQUIPMENT

Heat-resistant gloves

Face mask with suitable smoke-fume filter

1 Sawdust firing
Prepare your sawdust "kiln". First, make a platform from brick to protect the ground beneath from scorching. You can construct the kiln from ordinary clay house bricks, but avoid cement bricks, as cement can break up in extreme heat. When making any type of kiln it is vital that you ensure it is a stable structure that cannot be easily knocked over. Ensure that the brick structure is stacked securely by placing the brick layers over the joins of the lower layer, thus "locking" the wall together. This is very important, especially at the corners, because stacking the bricks directly on top of each other will make a less stable, and therefore potentially dangerous, kiln. This kiln has six bricks on each layer. When you have built up four layers of bricks, fill half of the kiln with dry sawdust and shavings. Wearing heat-resistant gloves, take the pre-heated pot from the kiln or oven and place it into the sawdust.

2 A sawdust kiln can be made from a metal container such as a bucket or garbage bin (dustbin), providing there is nothing combustible on it such as plastic handles or paint. Here a metal bucket is made more stable by surrounding it with bricks. When packing the kiln ensure there is at least 3 in. (8 cm.) of the dry sawdust all around the pot. If more than one piece is fired at a time, you can place wire mesh in between the layers (though this is only necessary with larger, heavier pots). Cover the pot with more sawdust and shavings. It is important to fill the kiln to the top with sawdust/shavings, as otherwise the gap will provide too much oxygen space, resulting in the sawdust burning cleanly rather than "charcoaling". Place crumpled dry newspaper on top of the sawdust.

3 Set fire to the crumpled paper. Get a strong flame established. Put on protective flame-retardant gloves (welder's gloves work well) and a face mask with suitable fume filter.

4 When the flames have died down, check to see that the sawdust itself is burning. If not, add more paper to the fire. Place a non-flammable lid on top of the kiln (an old metal baking tray is used here as the lid for the bucket, and a large kiln shelf is used to cover the brick kiln). This will put out the flames and create thick smoke.

WARNING

Sawdust is an extremely combustible material. Do not allow it to become airborne, especially near flame as this is potentially explosive.

Sawdust must be stored safely. If in doubt seek advice.

Sawdust firings will create some smoke and possibly flying embers from the burning paper and sawdust. Therefore, do not build and fire sawdust kilns in any area where this may cause a hazard to people or animals, or in any area where it could cause a fire. For example, sawdust firing is unsuitable for dry grassy or forest areas which are at risk from fire. The sawdust kiln must be located well away from anything which could catch fire or be damaged by heat. You should also ensure that there are no burning restrictions for the area. If in any doubt you *must* seek further advice.

Always wear a face mask with suitable smoke fume filter when you are dealing with smoke.

The sawdust kiln will become extremely hot, and you must ensure that children, animals, and anybody or anything else at risk are kept away until the kiln has cooled down.

The soot and ash from the firing must also be disposed of carefully to prevent fire or health risk. Beware that there may be burning embers left in the sawdust even though it may seem to be cold.

All pots fired in a sawdust kiln will be unsuitable for food or liquid.

5 Adjust the lid to allow some oxygen into the kiln, taking note of the wind conditions (see notes bottom right). It is important to hold down metal lids with bricks so the wind does not knock them off during the firing.

6 The time the sawdust firing takes will vary, but usually 24 hours is sufficient time for small kilns. If the kiln is still smoking, or if the sides are too hot to touch, it is not finished. When the kiln has cooled down completely, put on protective heat-resistant gloves, remove the lid, and lift out your pot, which can then be gently rubbed down to remove excess ash.

SOME TIPS ON FIRING SAWDUST KILNS

There are many variables with sawdust firing, each contributing to the final results. The main variables and their results are as follows:

Shavings

Sawdust and wood shavings need to be dry for sawdust firing.

If you use only fine sawdust, it may be difficult to combust due to lack of oxygen between the dust particles, so you may need to mix it with dry wood shavings, which are coarser.

If, however, you use mainly coarse sawdust or shavings, there may be too much oxygen in the mix, resulting in the sawdust mixture giving results similar to an electric kiln firing, rather than leaving carbonized black surfaces on your pots. Experiment to find the best mix to suit your firings. Beautiful effects can be obtained by deliberately placing wood shavings at one side of the pot for a "clean" burn while the other side of the piece has "charcoaling" sawdust to make a jet-black surface, thus creating an interesting pattern. Likewise, non-combustible shapes, for example made from clay, can be tied around the pot with wire to create a resist pattern.

The air gaps on the kiln

Just as the amount of oxygen within the sawdust mixture is important, so too is the amount of oxygen able to reach the sawdust.

There must be a small amount of air circulation to prevent the charcoaling embers from extinguishing. This is best achieved by leaving a small gap between the lid and the sawdust. If, however, there is too much of a gap, again the sawdust will burn and not "charcoal." If you are using corrugated iron for the lid of your sawdust kiln, it may be necessary to fill some of the gaps with soft clay. Larger sawdust kilns may need air gaps in the lower wall of the kiln, as larger amounts of sawdust will require more oxygen to fire, and the air holes at the bottom of the kiln will draw the burning down to reach the base. With brick kilns this can be achieved by leaving small gaps between a few of the bricks, or if you have bricks with holes in them, these can be turned to use the holes. If these allow too much oxygen in them they can be filled with soft clay.

With metal garbage bin (dustbin) kilns it may be necessary to put two or three holes of about 1¼ in. (3 cm.) diameter near the base. You can buy specially adapted incinerator bins which already have holes in the wall and a chimney hole in the lid, but you will need to block off most of the holes with soft clay before firing.

Weather conditions

It is best to avoid sawdust firing in very windy or rainy conditions. Light breezes afford the ideal conditions because these will "feed" the sawdust embers with oxygen as well as help to disperse the smoke.

The amount of wind or breeze will have to be taken into account when deciding how much of an air gap to leave on the lid, and any holes in the kiln walls (i.e. a smaller gap in breezy conditions and a slightly larger gap in calm conditions).

Just as there is undoubted pleasure in pinching flesh, making a pinch pot is very enjoyable – and in this case you inflict no pain. The desire to touch soft clay is almost irresistible, and there is the added attraction that, unlike flesh, it will retain the shape made with your fingers.

At its most basic, this method requires only your hands and some clay, so it is an excellent way to begin making. The simple action of gently squeezing soft clay between thumb and forefinger as the pot is slowly rotated in your hands can produce fine result.

Like shaking hands with a new acquaintance, making pinch pots will introduce you to the nature of the clay you are working with. You will feel its texture, which may be gritty or smooth, and more importantly, you will become aware of its wetness or dryness. The water content of the clay is vital. Too much water makes it sticky; too little and it will be hard and prone to cracking. Ideally you want to start with a piece of clay that is soft without being sticky.

While you are forming the piece, the warmth from your hands will begin to dry the clay, changing its character from soft and floppy to stiff and rigid. Often, however, the clay does not dry quickly enough, so it is advisable to work on two or three pots at a time, allowing the first to dry upside-down on plastic (to prevent the rims from drying).

Making the pots in rotation like this will teach you how quickly or slowly the clay dries, depending on the degree of heat and humidity of your working area. This discovery will give you a sense of timing that is vital in helping you with all of your clay work.

All clay-making techniques can be combined, for example, the "Red Pots" shown here were made by adding coils of clay onto pinch pots.

The three pinch pot projects that follow show basic making techniques, which can be adapted to your own designs and ideas.

Tina Vlassopulos
*"Red Pots." red earthenware pinched with
added-on coils, scraped back and burnished.
Fired to 1725°F (940°C).*

Priscilla Mouritzen
*Pinched bowls. Manganese
dioxide and iron oxide painted
on and incised.*

Micki Schloessingk
*Pinched spoons. Stoneware clay. "Salt
fired" (see glossary).*

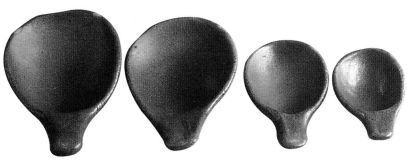

PINCHING

John Ward
*Green and white disc pot. Flattened coils
added onto a pinch pot. Stoneware with
painted oxides.*

Michael Flynn
*"Harlequin." Coiled and
pinched stoneware. "Raku"
fired and smoked in
sawdust.*

MATERIALS

I lb. (450 g.) Soft, well-prepared, heavily grogged "raku"-type clay

4 tablespoons water

EQUIPMENT

Metal spoon

FURTHER INFORMATION

For explanation of unfamiliar words and technical terms, refer to the Glossary on pages 138–141

LIDDED PINCH POT

This project, which is to be sawdust fired (see pp.27–29), is specially designed for anyone who is itching to make pots but does not have access to a kiln. If you do have a high-temperature kiln, or access to one, it is advisable to bisque fire the pots to 1830°F (1000°C) prior to sawdust firing as this will minimize breakage during the firing and make the finished piece more durable – though still unsuitable for food or liquid use.

A heavily grogged "raku" type of clay has been selected for its ability to withstand more thermal shock than smoother clays. If you have a smooth clay, you can add up to 10% fine silica sand or grog. The gritty nature of the clay will also make it dry more quickly, so you may need to keep your hands damp while working, though avoid making the clay wet and thus sticky. If, however, the pot is soft and sagging, leave it upside-down to dry a little.

1 Begin with a ball of prepared clay that is soft but not sticky. The ball should be small enough to fit comfortably in one hand, and the surface should be smooth, as any folds could develop into cracks later on.

2 **Hollowing out**
Holding the ball of clay in one hand, press your thumb into the center to begin hollowing it out (pinch pots are sometimes called "thumb pots"). Beware of using too much pressure, as this would result in a thin spot or even a hole in the wall of the pot.

3 Rotate the pot in one hand while you gently pinch the clay wall to approximately ⅜ in. (5 mm.) thick. Work from the base of the pot upwards, ensuring that the walls do not vary in thickness, but are smooth and uniform. Leave a thick rim on top, as this will prevent the rim from drying too quickly and then cracking.

4 Pinch the opening of the pot outwards to make a larger aperture, or squeeze inwards, as shown here, to make the opening smaller. Without making the top rim too thin, pinch up to form the gallery which the lid will fit over.

5 To make the lid, take a smaller ball of soft clay and follow steps 1 through 4 with a more gentle touch. When the lid is a little drier than leatherhard rub the back of a spoon on the surface to burnish it (see Burnishing, page 42).

The pot has the characteristic black carbonized surface. No water was used to clean it because the temperature of the sawdust firing in the small bucket probably only reached a few hundred degrees – not a high enough temperature to ensure it would not return to soft clay if immersed in water, and the pot was not bisque (biscuit) fired first.

6 **Drying**
When the pot is finished, allow it to dry completely before firing. The amount of drying time will depend on the temperature and humidity. One test of dryness is to hold the pot to your cheek; if it feels cool it is not yet dry. Refer to pages 27–29 for sawdust firing.

MATERIALS

Clay work

4 lbs. (1.8 kg.) stoneware clay

¼ cup water or slip for joins

TOOLS

Brush

Pointed wooden stick (knitting needle or long-handled paint brush)

Mesh for surface texture

Needle

Foam or cloth support

Rolling pin

Knife

Implements for impressed pattern-making

Glazing

Latex resist

Soap

Paint brushes

Sponge

Underglaze colors

EQUIPMENT

Firing cones 03, 7, 8, 9, 10

Kiln

Rubber gloves

FURTHER INFORMATION

For explanation of unfamiliar words and technical terms, refer to the Glossary on pages 138–141

MONSTER MONEY BOX

This piece is designed to show how to join different pieces of clay together, and how to introduce textured surface detail. It also demonstrates a method of making a cone shape by using a pointed wooden stick. This is another way of creating a hollow vessel from a solid piece of clay. The stick is used to thin the inside wall in a shape that would be too narrow for fingers, and could also be used to make other shapes such as teapot spouts.

For the Monster Money Box, there are many different shapes to be assembled, which requires the clay to be dried to the correct state. If it is too soft the shapes will distort during assembly, and if allowed to become drier than leatherhard, the joins will crack. Learning to catch the clay at just the right state to work on is one of the most important lessons in ceramics. Generally the best joins are made when both pieces of clay are in the same state of wet or dry, and as soft as possible.

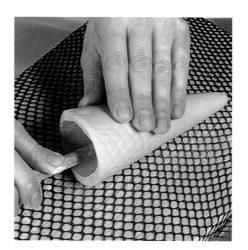

1 Making the shapes
Make a solid cone shape from the clay, then place a sharpened stick into the center of the thick end and push it down to within ⅝ in. (15 mm.) of the point of the cone. Thin the wall by rolling the cone over a textured surface, using the skewer inside to push the clay around.

2 When the wall of the cone is about ⅜ in. (5 mm.) thick take out the wooden skewer and gently curve the cone to form the tail of the monster. Score the top edge with a needle in a crosshatch pattern.

3 Make a rounded cylinder pinch pot (see p.32) for the upper torso of the monster. The opening must be the same diameter as the cone. Score its edge with a needle in a crosshatch pattern, then apply water or slip to both of the scored edges.

4 **Joining the shapes**
If the clay is too soft, leave it to dry with the scored ends down on plastic to prevent the edges from drying. After applying water to both scored edges, stick the two pinch pots together and smooth the join over, taking care not to smear too much of the surface texture.

5 Place the body of the monster to dry on a support of foam or crumpled cloth, then make the legs from small pinch pots, leaving the feet solid for more strength. When the body is dry enough to hold its shape, cut holes where the legs are to be joined, then score the surfaces, add water or slip and join two legs securely onto the body.

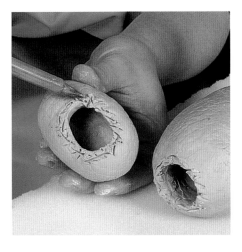

6 Make a pinch-pot head and join it on in the same way. Ensure that the hole between the head and body is large enough to accommodate the coins which will be inserted into the mouth and drop down into the stomach. Remember that the clay will shrink by about 10% during drying and firing.

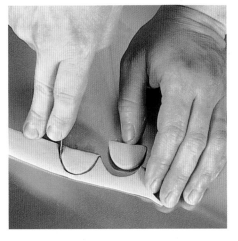

7 **Adding detail**
Again leave the monster to dry supported on its side, until it is stiff enough to safely stand on its two legs and tail, but be careful not to let it dry past the leatherhard stage. Roll out a small slab of clay, and cut semi-circle shapes to make the spine crests.

8 The crest shapes can be given detail by pressing various objects into the clay. Here the pointed end of a bottle opener is used to press a star pattern. Turn the crest over and repeat, taking care to use gentle pressure on the reverse side to avoid damaging the pattern on the front.

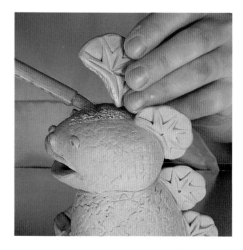

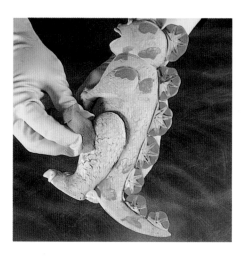

9 Join on the crest shapes, taking care not to spoil the impressed pattern. Make the thin arms from solid clay. Separate claws of soft clay can be added for extra detail, then the arm should be scored, wetted and securely joined on. A ravioli pasta cutter can be used to add more surface texture. Leave the monster to dry completely before bisque (biscuit) firing.

10 Highlighting the textured surface
After bisque firing, paint on latex resist to the base of the pot and any areas you wish to remain white. Brush on underglaze colors (see p.16) all over the surface. **Remember, all underglaze and glaze materials are toxic until glazed and fired!**

11 Wearing plastic gloves, use a damp but not wet sponge to lightly take off the top layer of color. Rinse the sponge frequently, wringing out most of the water. The underglaze color will remain in the deeper recesses of the surface texture. The pot must be left to dry for at least a day.

LATEX

Latex, a liquid that dries to a rubbery consistency, can be applied to both greenware and bisqued pots to resist decoration or glaze. It is applied thickly and left to dry (it turns from milky white to clear when dry), then is peeled off after decorating or glazing to reveal the clean surface beneath. To prevent the latex from drying and spoiling your brush, put your brush into liquid soap or dishwashing liquid before dipping it into the latex. Rinse the brush in water and re-soap it seven or eight minutes.

12 Glazing
Carefully pour glaze down the monster's mouth. A dark blue glaze is used here (recipe p.17). Swirl the glaze round inside and then quickly pour it back into its container; the glaze should not be inside the pot for more than a few seconds.

13 Hold the monster by its head and dip it up to its neck into well-stirred green glaze (see p.17) for three seconds – no more. Do not allow the glaze to go in its mouth.

15 Use a brush to fill in any bare patches with glaze. When the glaze has dried, wear a face mask with a dust filter and carefully rub down any doubly thick areas of glaze or glaze drips. Remove the latex resist. Use a needle to pull up the edge of the latex and then dispose of it safely as it will be covered in toxic underglaze and glaze.

The shiny green glaze was made by adding 2% copper oxide and ¼% cobalt oxide to a purchased transparent stoneware glaze. The transparency of the glaze has allowed the underglaze color to show through. The pot was bisque (biscuit) fired to 2012°F (1100°C) and glaze fired to 2336°F (1280°C).

14 Pour the well-stirred glaze into a smaller container that enables you to see the pot clearly when dipping the head. Holding the glazed body, dip the top of the head into the glaze for two seconds only. Once again take care not to allow the glaze into the monster's mouth.

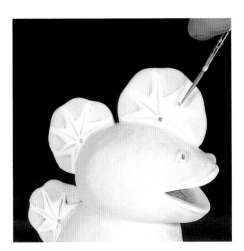

16 **Final details**
Wipe any remaining glaze off the base with a damp sponge. Ensure that no glaze is left on any surface that will touch the kiln shelf. Highlight details on the unglazed areas, like the claws, eyes and centers of the spine crests by brushing on underglaze color before glaze firing (see pp.23–24).

MATERIALS

1 lb. (450 g.) porcelain clay

Water or slip

Wax resist

Glaze (see p. 52 for application)

Ink

TOOLS

Balloon

Plastic bag or other support

Plastic wrap

Rolling pin

Potter's knife

Needle

Rubber gloves

EQUIPMENT

High temperature kiln

Firing cones 03 and 7, 8, 9, 10

FURTHER INFORMATION

For explanation of unfamiliar words and technical terms, refer to the Glossary on pages 138–141

PIERCED PORCELAIN POTPOURRI POT

Making pinch pots over supports, such as inflated plastic bags or balloons with plastic wrap draped over it to prevent sticking enables you to create delicate shapes which would collapse if made in the hand. The clay shape can fold around the balloon and remain on it until dry. Cracking is prevented by releasing air from the balloon as the pot dries and shrinks. Before firing, burst the balloon and remove it and the plastic wrap from the pot.

When making the foot ring, choose the diameter and height of the stem foot carefully. Too narrow a foot ring will make the pot unstable, while very wide foot rings make even the thinnest pots look heavy. You may need to make several to find the size that looks right to you. Paper templates can be used to experiment with sizes.

A glaze which crazes has been chosen deliberately. After the glaze firing, ink is rubbed into the surface and then wiped away. The fine crazing lines absorb the ink, thus highlighting the pattern. Any color ink can be used, as can natural dyes such as tea. The crazing lines make the pottery unsuitable for food or drink.

PIERCED DECORATION

Use fine dentist's drill bits, small wood screws, or a sharp potter's knife point to make pierced and incised decoration. It is advisable to practice piercing on a test piece first. Always wear a face mask with suitable dust filters when working with clay dust. Piercing can also be done on bisque-fired (biscuit-fired) ware.

Rolling pin and hole-cutter

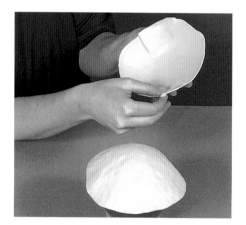

1 **Make the shape**
Take a ball of porcelain and pinch a bowl shape as shown on page 32. When the pot becomes floppy, place it over the inflated balloon support to dry. Fold up the plastic wrap around the rim of the pot to prevent the rim from drying.

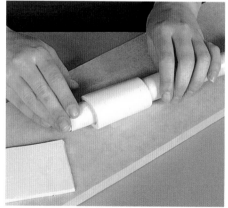

2 **Make the stem foot**
Roll out a small slab of clay, and follow the procedures for making napkin rings on page 66. The foot ring should be joined on before the bowl has dried to the leatherhard stage. The balloon will support the soft pot, preventing distortion.

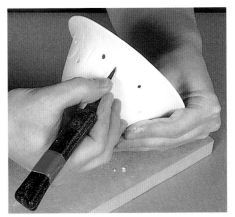

3 Join on the stem foot
Score and wet the edge of the foot ring, place it centrally on the pot, then lift it. The wet mark will show you where to score a crosshatch pattern. Apply slip and join the foot ring securely. Small coils of clay can be added if the join needs reinforcing.

4 Finishing details
When the bowl is leatherhard, pinch the walls into the final shape. If the rim feels dry, brush on water, waiting until it is absorbed before continuing. With your dust filter face mask on, decorate the bowl when it is dry by piercing holes through the walls and incising the surface.

After bisque (biscuit) firing to 2012°F (1100°C), the glaze was applied thickly to give crazing lines throughout the surface (for glaze dipping, see p.103). The glaze was made by adding 10% yellow stain to a transparent glaze which fires to 2336°F (1280°C), see pp. 16–19. Note the stained glass effect where the glaze fills the pierced decoration.

Unlike pinch pots, which tend to be limited in scale, coiled pots can be as large as you like because they are made from units of clay rather than just one initial lump. Coils can be added to any clay work providing the clay is soft enough, and even wheel-thrown pots can be enlarged by adding coils to the rim. In one of the projects in this section you will see how a pinch pot is enlarged with coiling.

The individual coils can be made in various different ways from hand rolling to mass production through a pug mill. The process can also be done using lengths of flat slab. The thickness required for the coils will depend on the size of the work. They should be approximately twice the thickness of the intended final wall to allow for the joining process. If your coils are too thin the joins between the layers will be weak and prone to cracking.

To ensure strong joins, the clay must also be soft, so when making coils it is important to start with soft clay and take care not to overwork it, as warm hands will dry it. Absorbent surfaces should be dampened, and if coils are not to be used immediately, they should be placed on plastic sheets and covered to prevent them drying.

To make a strong join between layers of coils, the top layer of clay must be pulled down to mix with the bottom layer. Beware of just pinching the coil thinner when you place it on, as this will not join the layers properly, and they are likely to come apart when dry. For most coil pots, the lower sections will need to dry and stiffen before more coils are added, or the walls may collapse. During drying, the top rim must always be kept soft by covering it with plastic wrap (cling film).

The process of coiling results in a distinctive surface pattern showing the marks made by the repeated process of pulling the clay down to join the layers together. This texture can be retained or scraped smooth. Other textures, or impressed patterns, can be applied to the pot before the clay surface is dry.

Above: **Barbara Swarbrick** Bowl. Earthenware clay, slab-built with coiled additions. Underglaze decoration.
Top left: **Judy Trim** Bowl. Coil-built, colored slips applied and burnished, with subsequent luster decoration.

Fiona Salazar
*"Black Pot." Stoneware
and white earthenware
clays mixed, coil-built,
painted on colored slip,
burnished, fired to
1740°F (950°C).*

Alan Heaps
*"Lovers." Slab-built with press-
molded shapes and coils added.*

COILING

**Liam Curtin and
Wendy Jones**
Tin glaze. Majolica
decoration on press
molded platter.

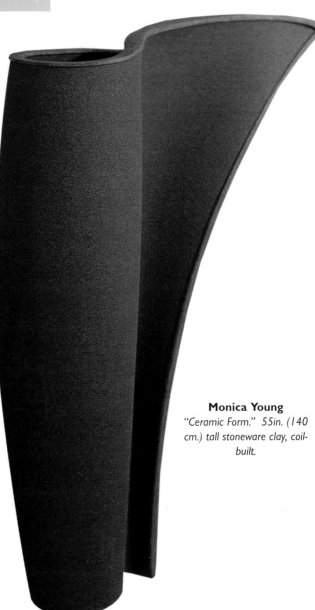

Monica Young
*"Ceramic Form." 55in. (140
cm.) tall stoneware clay, coil-
built.*

MATERIALS

5 lbs. (2.25 kg.) smooth red earthenware
clay

¼ cup (50 ml.) each of colored slip – light
blue, dark blue, green, yellow

Plastic wrap

Water

Low-temperature glaze 1742°F (950°C)

TOOLS

Needle

Brush for water and slip

Wooden paddle stick (optional)

Metal scraper

Potter's knife

Pointed modeling tool

Shapes for impressed pattern for inlay

Metal spoon with smooth back
(or polished pebble)

Rubber gloves

EQUIPMENT

Small board

Flat surface for rolling coils

Banding wheel (optional)

Firing cones 09, 08, 07

FURTHER INFORMATION

For explanation of unfamiliar words and
technical terms, refer to the Glossary on
pages 138–141

TO HAND-ROLL COILS

Take about 1 lb. (450 g.) of prepared soft
clay (see p.10) and squeeze it into a
rounded length. Taper the ends to
prevent the clay from forming hollow
coils as you roll it forward and backward
on a damp flat surface. Use your
fingertips spread wide and moving along
the length of the coil to avoid thick and
thin lumps. Apply less pressure at the
start of each forward and backward
movement, as this will prevent the coils
from becoming flattened.

BURNISHED AND DECORATED VASE

This vase begins with a coil of clay spiralled around to make the base. Coils are then placed on the outer edge of the rim to make the shape wider, then on the inner edge to narrow it.

Smooth red earthenware clay has been selected for this project, both for its rich color and suitability for burnishing. This is a slow process; burnishing the whole surface while it dries will take many hours, but the resulting lustrous sheen is well worth the effort. The reason for choosing a glaze that melts at 1742°F (950°C) is that burnishing will become dull if fired at a higher temperature. The glaze is decorative rather than functional, as it is prone to crazing, and the vase will therefore not be waterproof. A small cup can be placed inside it to hold water when it is used for fresh flowers.

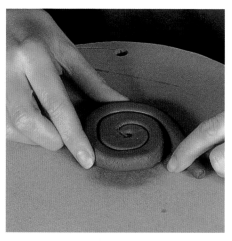

1 Making the base
Roll out coil lengths, but only make a few coils to prevent them from drying out (or make more and wrap them in plastic). If the coils become dry and crack when bent in a curve, then start again with softer clay and work on a damp surface.

2 Place a small wooden board on your banding wheel and roll the first coil into a tight spiral on the board. If you do not have a banding wheel you can simply turn the board around on the tabletop as you work.

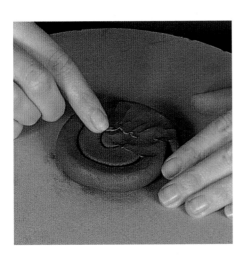

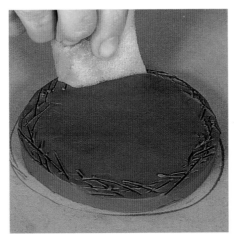

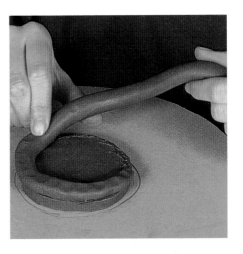

3 Use your index finger or thumb to smear the top layer of clay from the outer edge towards the center, thereby securely joining the coil length. If the clay is not dragged across the top surface the coil will crack apart when drying. Turn it over and repeat on the reverse side.

4 Tension the base by pressing it with your hand or a flat tool, then score the edge with a needle in a crosshatch pattern, and use a brush or sponge to wet the edge. This needs to be repeated each time a new layer of coils is applied.

5 Building the wall
Press a coil of clay on the wet scored edge. The coil can continue around further than one layer, but it is easier to control the shape if you pinch off the coil where it completes the perimeter of the shape.

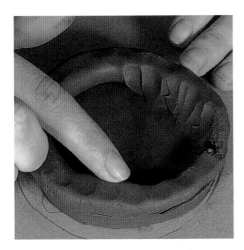

6 Using your thumb or finger, drag down the edge of the coil to the base on the inside of the pot and then again on the outside. Dragging the surface of the clay downwards is essential for making strong joins between the coils. This process will thin the coil by approximately a half.

7 To make the shape wider, place the coil on the outer edge of the pot and join securely as before. Beware of placing the coil on the edge and merely pinching it thinner – this does not make a secure join and results in cracking.

8 Shape and surface
The walls can be thinned, shaped, and given texture or pattern by using any suitable object for hitting the surface. Support the wall with your other hand inside the pot to prevent pushing it out of shape. You can hold a smooth pebble against the inside wall to assist the thinning process.

9 Leave the pot to dry with its rim covered in plastic wrap to keep it soft. When the clay walls are leatherhard (see p.15), unwrap the top edge, score with a needle and wet as before. To narrow the shape, place the coil on the inner edge of the rim.

10 Use a metal scraper to scrape down the surface, smoothing it in preparation for burnishing. On other coil pots you may wish to keep the distinctive pattern from the repeated joining process, or add texture.

11 **Trimming the top**
Use the end of your metal scraper to mark out the undulating shape of the rim, then cut it out with your potter's knife. Dip your thumb and index finger in water and run them around the undulating rim to smooth down the cut edges. Incise a line around both the upper and lower edges with a pointed modeling tool.

12 **Slip inlay and brushed pattern**
Dip paper cutouts in water and place them on the vase to evenly space the pattern. Use small stamps, like this wooden chopstick with its end cut to a semi-circle, to impress pattern 1/16 in. (2 mm.) deep for slip inlay.

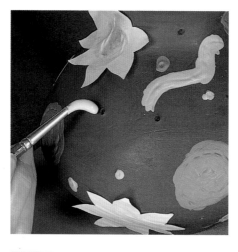

13 Brush colored slips into the impressed pattern. As the slip dries it will shrink, so you will have to apply more layers of thick slip until you are certain it has filled the impressed pattern to the top.

14 When the slip has dried to leatherhard, scrape the surface with a metal scraper to remove the layer of colored slip and thus reveal the inlay pattern. Be careful not to scrape too deeply as this could remove all of the inlay.

15 To make additional patterns, brush on colored slip, applying it in two layers to ensure a good cover. When the slip has dried to leatherhard, scratch through with a pointed modeling tool to reveal the red earthenware clay underneath. This method is called sgraffito.

16 Burnishing
Burnish the surface by rubbing it with the smooth back of a spoon or a polished pebble. If the slip is not dry leatherhard, the pattern will smear, but if too dry the surface will be harder to burnish. Continue burnishing until the pot is completely dry. Plastic wrap wrapped around your finger can help with the final polishing.

After bisque (biscuit) firing to 1742°F (950°C), latex resist was carefully painted around the underside of the rim. When it was dry, the glaze was applied (see p.134). The latex was then removed, leaving the outside of the vase unglazed. The glaze was made by adding 2% cobalt to a transparent glaze which fires to 1742°F (950°C).

MATERIALS

6 lbs. (2.7 kg.) White stoneware clay

Water

Prepared underglaze colors – yellow, red, green, blue, crimson purple, brown

Transparent stoneware glaze

TOOLS

Needle

Brushes

Rubber (optional) and metal scrapers

Surform blade (optional)

Home-made cut plastic template for shaping stem foot rim

EQUIPMENT

Banding wheel (optional)

Board

Flat surface for rolling coils

Garden spray bottle (optional)

Large jug

Face mask with dust filter

Firing cones 03 and 02, 01, 1

Kiln

Rubber gloves

FURTHER INFORMATION

For explanation of unfamiliar words and technical terms, refer to the Glossary on pages 138–141

Large and small scrapers with two fine brushes

OVAL FRUIT BOWL ON STEM FOOT

For this project the shape begins with a pinch pot, to which coils are added. The oval is an introduction to the endless possibilities of non-circular forms that can be made by the coiling process. Coiling is also one of the best methods for making non-symmetrical shapes, whether abstract or figurative.

The fruit bowl has a stem foot added on after the bowl is made, which allows it to be much thinner and more delicate. If made first, it would have had to be thicker to support the weight of the bowl during making.

A white stoneware clay has been chosen to give a light background to the underglaze pattern. White stoneware is a strong plastic clay with fewer cracking problems than other white clays such as porcelains or white earthenware.

1 Beginning the shape
Make a thick pinch pot with walls ³⁄₈ in. (1 cm.) thick and dry it to leatherhard, keeping the rim soft with plastic wrap. A banding wheel will assist with the coiling process, but if you do not have one you can simply turn the pot around. Apply coil lengths to the scored and wet rim of the pinch pot and securely join as shown earlier. Do not allow the base to dry beyond the leatherhard stage; it can be wrapped in plastic to prevent over-drying.

2 Push the wall together to form an oval shape with an undulating rim, then build up with coils until the walls are too soft and floppy for further layers. Leave the pot to dry upside-down on plastic with its rim covered to stay soft. If preferred, the undulating rim can be levelled by adding coils to the lower dips, but in this case the shape has been retained.

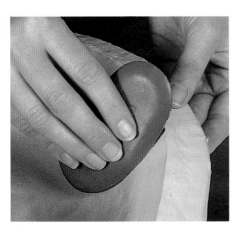

3 Forming the wide rim

When the wall of the pot is leatherhard, again score and wet the top edge before adding the next coil layer. Apply the coils to the outer edge of the rim to make a wide flattened rim to finish the top of the shape. Use a rubber scraper to smooth down the shape inside the bowl. Leave the pot to dry to leatherhard.

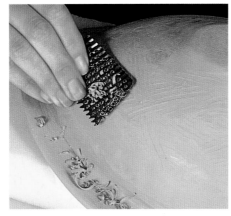

4

When leatherhard, turn the pot upside-down onto a foam support (or crumpled-up cloth). Scrape down any bumps on the surface. Use a Surform blade (normally used for shaving wood, but also good for leatherhard clay) or metal scraper, which can be toothed or smooth edged.

APPLYING UNDERGLAZE

It is best to apply underglaze colors at the leatherhard to dry stage. The unfired surface is less porous than bisque (biscuit) ware, so the liquid underglaze will paint on more smoothly. Another advantage is that the subsequent firing will fix the colors onto the clay, making them less likely to smudge during glazing. Always test the underglaze colors with the glaze, if you intend to use one, before applying them to your work. Some underglaze colors are prone to bubbling if applied too thickly, and so it is best to apply them thinly, much like watercolor paints. Thin layers can be built up, and many underglaze colors can be successfully mixed or over-layered, but you must test them first; being made from metal oxides, they are not like conventional paints, and give less predictable results.

The underglaze can be applied with anything from brushes, sponges and airbrushes to rags, using "rag rolling" methods. Providing the color is not used too thickly, it can be applied in almost any way imaginable, with each application implement giving its own distinctive texture.

Remember, underglaze colors are toxic and must not be inhaled, ingested or left on your skin.

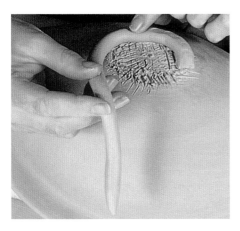

5 Making the stem foot

Decide where to place the stem foot. A banding wheel or throwing wheel will help you place the foot ring centrally, but otherwise use a ruler to mark out the center. Score and wet a crosshatch pattern, put a soft coil of clay onto the scored base, and continue applying and joining coils until the stem foot is the right size.

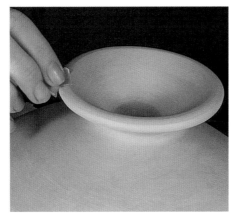

6

Smooth the surface and use a home-made plastic template to incise a line around the rim to define the edge. This shows exactly where to wipe the glaze off. Dry the stem foot to leatherhard. The pot is now ready to be decorated with underglaze colors. If your stem foot is too delicate to support the weight of the bowl, leave it upside-down to dry completely and then bisque (biscuit) fire the bowl first, keeping it upside-down during the firing. Underglaze colors can also be applied to bisque-fired pots.

7 **Applying underglaze colors**
Leave the pot to dry slowly until completely dry, then bisque (biscuit) fire to 1830°F (1000°C). Underglaze colors can be applied both at the leatherhard stage and after firing, so you can continue the underglaze painting or begin it now (see step 6). Paint fruit shapes on in thin layers using the different colors.

8 Build up the grapes from different layers of thin color, starting with a thin blue spiral painted on for each grape, followed by crimson, then a line of crimson mixed with blue lightly brushed on top. Use a needle to scratch (sgraffitto) a line through each shape. Note the glaze-fired underglaze test pieces.

9 Underglaze can also be bought in the form of pencils or chalks. These can be applied to the bisque (biscuit) ware in the same way you would use drawing materials. They smudge easily, but this could be used to advantage in order to achieve soft blends of color.

10 **Banding decoration**
Use a turntable/banding wheel if you have one, or alternatively a throwing wheel (see p.112). Spin the wheel with one hand while the other hand holds a brush dipped in color steady on the surface. Let the pot, not your brush, move around.

11 After applying wide brush strokes of blue underglaze on the top rim of the bowl, hold the flat side of the brush on the edge of the oval rim to apply a band of color. If you use the brush in this way you are less likely to go over the edge than if you use the cut end of the brush, where the hairs can separate.

12 **"Fixing" the underglaze**
If you have applied any underglaze to the bisque ware, it is a good idea to bisque fire again to "fire-in" the color and prevent it from smudging during glazing. Smudging is also less likely if you can dip the entire pot at once into a large container of glaze. Smaller amounts of glaze can be poured over. Minimize the risk of smudging by first spraying a thin layer of glaze onto the surface using an ordinary spray bottle.

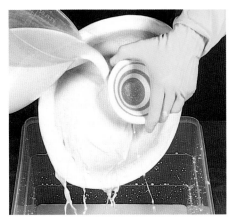

13 **Glazing by pouring**
Put the well-stirred transparent glaze (see pp.16–19) into a good pouring jug. The glaze should be just slightly thicker than the consistency of whole milk. Hold the bowl by its foot ring, taking care not to touch and smudge any unfired underglaze pattern, and quickly pour the glaze in.

14 As soon as the glaze is in the bowl, put down the jug and tip the glaze out of the bowl into a wide glaze container (the wider the better to catch any splashes). It is vital to do this while turning the bowl around so that the glaze pours out over each part of the rim and covers the whole inside and rim. This process should take no more than a few seconds or the glaze will build up too thickly. Avoid thick overlaps of glaze.

15 Now refill the jug with newly re-stirred glaze, hold the bowl over the glaze container, and pour the glaze over the outside, again avoiding thick overlaps. Finally, pour glaze into the stem foot and out again. If you miss any small areas these can be filled in with a brush full of glaze afterwards. Sponge the glaze off the foot ring.

After rubbing down any thick layers of glaze, the pot was fired to 2084°F (1140°C). Although the stoneware clay is stronger if fired up to 2336°F (1280°C), the lower temperature ensures that the colors do not burn out in the firing.

MATERIALS

15 lbs. (6.8 kg.) well-prepared red
earthenware clay (see p.13)

Water

Glaze

Glaze stains

Latex resist (see p.36)

Soap

Cold wax emulsion

TOOLS

Rolling pin

Cloth to roll slab on (optional)

Cloth or plastic to pick up lid

Cloth to make hammock for lid doming

Needle

Knife

Brushes

Rubber or metal scrapers

Sponge

Toothbrush

EQUIPMENT

Clay extruder (optional)

Flat board

Cardboard box for lid shaping

Kiln

Firing cones 06 and 03, 02, 01, 1

Rubber gloves

FURTHER INFORMATION

For explanation of unfamiliar words and
technical terms, refer to the Glossary on
pages 138–141

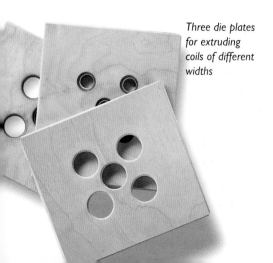

*Three die plates
for extruding
coils of different
widths*

BREAD BIN

This bread bin combines coiling with two other hand building techniques, pinching and slabbing (see pp.56–59). It begins with a slab base, because large flat bases made from slab will have fewer cracking problems than those made from a spiralled coil of clay.

The coils are deliberately thick – ⅝ in. (15 mm.) – partly to allow for strong joins on the large-scale object, but also to give spare clay thickness on the walls, enabling light pinching to enlarge and shape the pot after the coils have been joined.

The coils can be extruded, hand rolled, or made with a hand "coiler" tool. This is simply a steel loop firmly fixed to a handle, which you drag through a long length of well-prepared solid clay. The steel loop cuts a coil through the block of clay.

Red earthenware clay is the traditional clay used for tin-glaze majolica decoration.

1 Making coils
If you have an extruder, select or make a round die plate with a ⅝ in. (15 mm.) diameter hole and extrude coils, keeping them soft by placing them on plastic and wrapping them up. Otherwise, roll out the coils by hand as shown earlier (see page 42), or use a "hand coiler" tool as explained in the introduction.

2 Beginning with a slab base
Make a slab ¼ in. (6 mm.) thick and cut out the base of your bread bin (see p.56 for slab rolling). You can cut out a paper template for the base shape or use a ruler. Score and wet the top outer rim before placing it on the first coil.

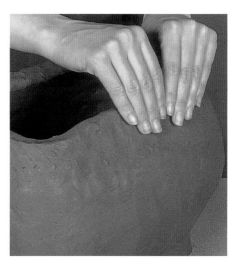

3 Building up the walls
Securely join the coil to the slab base by dragging a layer of the clay down, using your thumb or finger in a repeated downward motion around the entire perimeter of the shape. The coils have been made thick to allow for strong joins and to give enough spare clay to lightly pinch the walls a little thinner as you build the bin taller.

4 A rubber or metal scraper can be used to smooth both the inside and the outside of the bin. If you find any large dips in the surface, these can be plugged with soft clay and smoothed over. When smoothing the inside of the shape you should also gently curve and widen the walls.

5 When the walls of the bin become difficult to control due to the softness of the clay, leave the bin to dry until leatherhard, keeping the top rim soft by covering it with plastic. Then continue adding and joining coils, which can be pinched taller and thinner as you work up the side of the bin.

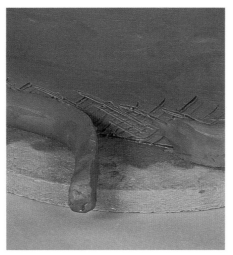

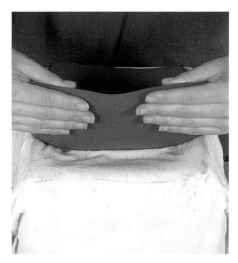

6 Forming the gallery
When the bin is the height you want, join on a coil to the inside of the rim to form the gallery, which the lid will rest on. Smooth down this coil, taking care to make the edge rounded, as this will prevent chipping when the bread bin is in use.

7 Adding decorative edges
A thick coil of clay cut in half lengthwise can be joined on both the base and top of the bin as an optional decorative rim. Score the bin in a crosshatch pattern and wet with water or slip and press the half coil firmly on to make a strong join. Avoid making this coil more than ⅜ in. (1 cm.) thick, or it could crack.

8 Making the lid
Roll out a slab of clay ³/₁₆ in. (5 mm.) thick and cut out a rectangle with rounded corners at least ¾ in. (3 cm.) wider all around than the size of the opening on the bread bin. Make this slab into a dome shape by placing it in a "hammock" made from cloth taped over a cardboard box and leaving it there until leatherhard.

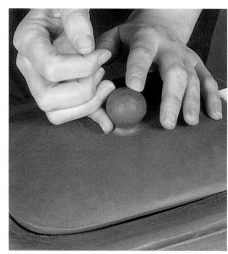

9 When leatherhard, trim the edge until it fits the bread bin. Check the fit by trying it out in position. To do this, put the lid on a length of folded-over cloth (or newspaper or plastic sheet), and pick it up by the cloth "handles" (without the cloth the lid would be difficult to remove from the bin). Ensure that the lid and the bin are the same level of dryness to prevent one from shrinking more than the other as it dries.

10 **Making the knob**
Make a small hollow pinch pot for the knob, then score and wet both the lid and knob with a needle before securely joining. Use the needle again to puncture a hole right through the knob and lid, either from the top or from underneath, to allow air to escape from the knob as it dries.

GLAZING LARGE POTS

To glaze the bread bin, first pour glaze inside the pot then quickly out again, as shown on pages 49 and 135. If you have an insufficient quantity of tin glaze to dip the outside of the bread bin, follow these steps. 1: Put a strong plank of wood across a wide glaze basin. 2: Place kiln props taller than the bread bin on top of the wooden plank. 3: Turn the bread bin upside-down over the props so that they support the bin at least ¾ in. (3 cm.) above the plank of wood. Now pour the well-stirred glaze over the bin, taking care to cover the entire surface.

MAJOLICA DECORATION

This term refers to the application of colored glaze stains to the surface on tin glaze. The glaze stains can be applied in any manner chosen, but must not be too thick or the surface may bubble during firing. Be careful not to brush over the surface more than twice, as repeated brushings not only produce a thick build-up, but also can remove the glaze layer. Some of the best majolica decoration is achieved by simply brushing the color onto the pot.

11 **Using latex resist**
It is best to apply majolica decoration soon after glazing before the surface becomes dry and powdery. Glaze the bin (see pp.48, 49, and 135), then put on a face mask with a dust filter and carefully rub down any drips or double layers of glaze. Paint on a latex resist pattern (see p.36) and leave it to dry (it will change from milky white to beige).

12 Brush yellow glaze stain on parts of the pattern, and sponge blue and green stains on other areas. Apply the stains thinly, with one stroke of the brush to avoid removing the thin glaze layer. Glazes should be tested before final use; note the glaze-fired test pieces below the bin.

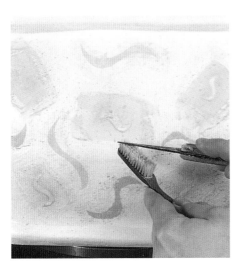

13 Red stain can now be lightly speckled on top of the yellow by dipping a toothbrush into the red stain then scraping the blade of a knife across the bristles to produce a random spatter.

14 Carefully peel away the latex layer, and dispose of it carefully as it will be covered in toxic glaze and stain dust. Any areas missed by the colored glaze stains can be filled in with a brush.

15 **Using cold wax resist** Cold wax emulsion, which acts in the same way as hot wax, is now applied over the top of the original colored stain pattern to protect it from the final layer of glaze. As with latex, protect your brushes by applying soap to them before putting them into the wax emulsion.

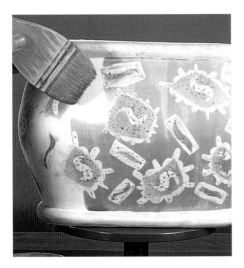

16 When the wax emulsion has completely dried, brush or sponge blue glaze stain over the surface. The way you apply the stain will show on the fired surface. The wax emulsion will resist most of the color, leaving only small drops which can be left on or wiped away with a damp sponge.

The base of the bread bin was sponged clean of glaze. The glaze was made by adding 8% tin oxide to a transparent glaze and fired to 2084°F (1140°C) (see pp.16–19). The pot had been bisque (biscuit) fired to 1830°F (1000°C).

A slab of clay is simply a flattened sheet, resembling a piece of pastry. There are ous ways of making slabs, and as with all making processes it is vital to experiment. Try making slabs by stretching the clay. Begin by flattening the clay to a thick slab, then pick it up, turn it over, and throw it down onto a flat surface with a sweeping motion of the arms. This will stretch the slab with every turning. Slabs can be rolled out with a pastry rolling pin, or at the other end of the scale, slab-rolling machines can be bought to speed up and mechanize the process. Slabs can also be made by cutting open the walls of a thrown cylinder and flattening the clay.

There are numerous different approaches to creating slabbed pots. The slabs can be used while they are still soft and flexible to create flowing organic forms, or they can be left to stiffen to the leatherhard stage and used to create crisp, straight-edged geometric shapes. They can be shaped by hand or pressed into or onto molds; the surface of the slab can be smooth or textured in any way chosen; materials such as grog or colored clays can be rolled into the surface.

If you are using leatherhard slabs it is essential to ensure they do not dry beyond this stage, as any joins would be likely to crack. The length of time it takes to dry a slab to leatherhard will depend on the clay, the surface it is on, and the temperature and humidity of the room it is in.

Slab building suits both small- and large-scale work. Very large pieces can be made lighter and less prone to cracking by adding one third volume of wet paper pulp to slip and then drying to plastic clay after mixing. This method, however, is unsuitable for kilns inside the home, as even very small pieces of paper burning off during firings can fill a room with dense, toxic smoke. Slow, even drying is needed to prevent cracking of the joins.

Above: **Judith Salomon** "Construction Bowl." White earthenware, slab-built, brushed-on colored glazes.
Top left: **Linda Chew** Oval quilt dish. Soft slabs impressed with textiles, cobalt oxide applied, unglazed.

Philomena Pretsell
*"Blue Frilly Jug." White earthenware clay,
slab built with impressed decoration.*

Janet Hamer
*"Ruddy Duck." Stoneware,
thrown and turned bowl, cut and
remodeled, slab-built head
and tail.*

SLABBING

Jutka Fischer
*Vases. White earthenware colored
with body stains, slabs made from
different colored clays with inlaid
decoration.*

Marion Brandis
*"Persian Fireplace." Buff earthenware,
slab-built sections, colored glazes
brushed on.*

MATERIALS

Well-prepared clay of your choice

1 cup (236 ml.) each of blue, light blue, green and yellow colored slip
(see pp. 14-15)

Cotton cloth for slab rolling (optional)

Various objects for impressed pattern (optional)

¼ oz. (5 g.) iron oxide (optional)

Rolling tobacco (optional)

Transparent or colored glazes
(see pp. 16-19)

TOOLS

Ruler

Rolling pin

Wooden strips for rolling guides

Potter's knife

Length of coil (optional)

Stamps and leaves for impressed patterns (optional)

Slip trailers

Sponge

Craft knife

EQUIPMENT

Flat wooden boards

Freezer (optional)

Flat mesh drying rack

Firing cones 8, 9 and 10 (stoneware), 06 and 03, 02, 01, 1 (earthenware)

Rubber gloves

Kiln

FURTHER INFORMATION

For explanation of unfamiliar words and technical terms, refer to the Glossary on pages 138–141

You can use a knife and a straightedge to cut tiles or invest in a tile cutter, like the one shown here

TILES

Making tiles provides an excellent opportunity to explore two major decorative areas – impressed texture and pattern, and slip decoration – both of which are capable of infinite variation. Stamps can be made from plaster, or bisque (biscuit) fired clay, but found objects can give exciting and often surprising results. Even crumpled newspaper rolled into the clay will create an interesting surface. Slip decoration also has endless possibilities. This project shows a few traditional slip techniques which you can develop. The cut-sponge decoration for printing slip (shown in step 11), can also be used to apply glaze, underglaze or enamel decoration in other projects.

If the finished tiles are to be fixed to internal walls, do not glaze the backs, as the porous clay gives stronger bonds. To make frost-proof tiles for outdoors, ensure that the tile is glazed all over with a craze-free glaze. This will ensure that no water can seep in which could freeze, expand and crack the glaze off. Fire these wholly glazed tiles on stilts, and after removing the stilts paint-varnish the stilt marks to waterproof them.

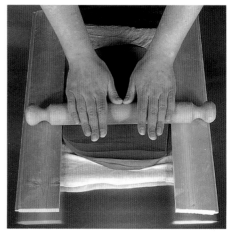

1 **Making slabs**
To roll out a slab, begin by flattening well-prepared clay with your hands on an absorbent surface. Make the flattened shape as even as possible, avoiding lumps. Cloth or paper helps to prevent the clay from sticking to the work bench or board.

2 Use a clean, dry, wooden rolling pin to further flatten the clay. Wooden guides of equal thickness can be used to help you roll the slab evenly. Use light pressure to roll the entire surface of the slab.

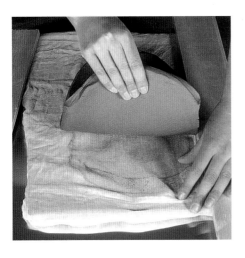

3 As the clay is pressed down, it sticks to the surface, thus preventing further stretching, so after every rolling, the slab must be picked up and turned over. You can pick up the cloth to assist with turning larger slabs. Continue until the rolled clay is between ¼ and ⅝ in. (6 and 15 mm.), as thinner tiles are more likely to warp.

4 Another way of making tiles is to begin with a solid block of soft, well-prepared clay and cut slabs from it using a wire stretched tightly between two sticks. The sticks have measured notches cut in them to give the different heights required. The ends of the sticks are dragged firmly across the flat surface to cut the tile flat.

5 **The great coil trick**
Decorative surfaces can be made by using a coil instead of a wire. The coils from old ring-bound notebooks work well, or you can wind coat-hanger wire around a broom handle for larger coils. Again begin with a block of soft, well-prepared clay

6 The coil can be pulled straight through, or for added pattern, pull it from left to right in a zigzag motion as you drag it through the clay. Then peel off the top layer to reveal two remarkably patterned surfaces.

7 **Cutting out plain tiles**
For plain, smooth-surfaced tiles let the slab dry to leatherhard before cutting it out. Tiles can be made singly or as panels. Here a tile panel is made by cutting through a slab in straight lines, but you can also cut interlocking asymmetric shapes.

8 **Pressing texture or pattern**
Begin with a soft slab for textured or patterned tiles. Leaves with strong shapes, such as ivy or cabbage, yield clear impressions when rolled into the clay and then removed. Do not fire the tiles with the leaves still on, as the slow burning would create unhealthy fumes.

9 Use soft slabs when making deep impressed patterns and make the slab thicker to allow for the extra thinning during the pressing of objects. You can make your own plaster or bisque-fired clay stamps, or use ready-made objects like this meat mallet. (Wooden kitchen implements should not be used for food again.)

10 **Cutting patterned tiles**
Due to the pressure of stamping pattern or texture on soft slab, the clay will stretch and distort, so if you want straight edges, the tiles must be cut after the pattern or texture has been pressed on. It is essential to smooth down the cut edges of all tiles by dipping your finger in water and lightly rubbing around them.

11 **Sponge decoration**
Synthetic sponges can be cut with a sharp craft knife or scissors. Freezing the damp sponge makes it much easier to cut. (Never use a hot wire to cut the sponge as this melts it and gives off toxic fumes.) Apply slip to the sponge and press it on the tile, which could have a different colored slip already brushed on and dry.

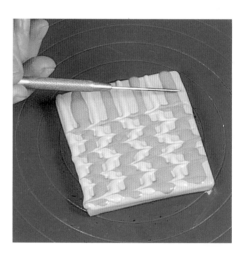

12 **Mocha decoration**
Make tobacco liquid by mixing rolling tobacco in a little boiling water and leaving it to soak overnight. Mix 2 tablespoons with $\frac{1}{4}$ teaspoon of iron oxide (brown) or manganese dioxide (darker brown/black) and strain the mixture through a 120-mesh sieve. Dip a leatherhard tile into well-stirred thick slip, then put one drop of the tobacco mix onto the wet slip.

13 **Feathering**
Hold the tile by its edges, dip it face down into well-stirred thick slip (about the consistency of heavy cream) leaving the back clean. Quickly slip trail lines of two contrasting-colors, taking care not to let the slip trailer nozzle touch the wet surface. Tap the tile to make the trailed lines sink into the wet surface.

14 Before the slips have dried, lightly trail through them with a thin point such as a needle. This will drag the colored slips together to produce a distinctive pattern, which was common in the 19th century.

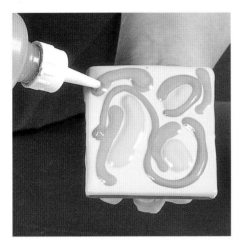

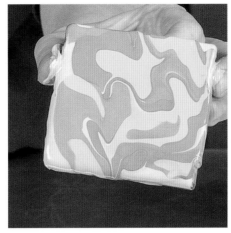

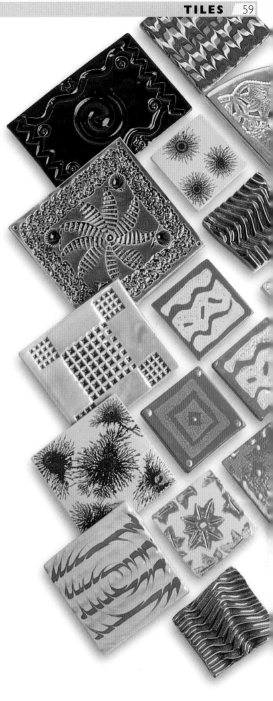

15 Marbling

As with feathering, begin by dipping the face of a leatherhard tile into well-stirred thick slip. Quickly, before the slip dries, slip trail contrasting colors in a random pattern. Here dark blue, green and yellow slips have been trailed on top of light blue.

16

Quickly, before the slips dry, shake and twist the tile to move the slip pattern on the surface. Be careful not to shake too hard as this could cause the entire surface to run off. Do not allow any drips to fall into your containers of single-colored slips.

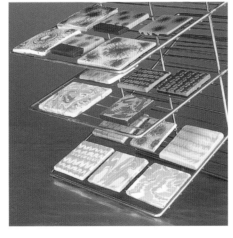

17

The marbled pattern can be left to dry, or you can feather the surface with a needle immediately after achieving the marbled pattern, providing it has not dried. Rather than straight lines, curved feathering lines are used here to emphasize the movement of the pattern.

18 Warping

Tiles can be made from any type of clay, though grogged clay is less prone to warping. It is essential to dry tiles slowly and evenly, as warping is caused by one surface drying and shrinking faster than the other. Flat open-mesh shelving will allow air to dry both sides of the tiles evenly and therefore reduce warping, otherwise turn tiles regularly when drying.

After bisque (biscuit) firing to 1830°F (1000°C), the slip decorated earthenware tiles were dipped into thin transparent glaze and fired to 2084°F (1140°C) on metal stilts. The stoneware tiles with impressed pattern were glazed in different colored stoneware glazes and fired to 2336°F (1280°C).

MATERIALS

5 lbs. (2.25 kg.) soft, well-prepared white stoneware clay

Paper for template

Cloth for rolling out slab (optional)

Water or slip for joining

¼ cup (50 ml.) blue slip (see p.14)

Plastic sheet

Light green transparent stoneware glaze (see p.17)

TOOLS

Scissors

Rolling pin

Potter's knife

Needle

Paint brush

EQUIPMENT

Flat board

Firing cones 06, 8, 9 and 10

Kiln

Rubber gloves

FURTHER INFORMATION

For explanation of unfamiliar words and technical terms, refer to the Glossary on pages 138–141

TOAST RACK OR LETTER RACK

For this rack, each upright could be made from a different freehand shape cut straight out of a slab without a template. If you prefer to make all of the uprights the same size and shape, you will find paper templates a great help. For identical shapes, cut through multiple layers of paper and place all of the required shapes on the slab to ensure there is enough space for all of them.

The shapes are to be cut from a slab of clay that is leatherhard. It is vital not to allow the clay to dry beyond this stage, so if in doubt, work with it a little softer. There will be less likelihood of joins cracking, than if you try to join clay when it is over-hard.

The glaze dipping can be done by holding the work with glazing tongs, or if you do not have these, hold the work with your thumb and finger as shown in step 6. With all glazes it is essential to have the glaze the correct thickness (see pp.16–19).

3 **Joining the shapes**
When all of the shapes have rounded edges with incised borders on both sides, use a needle to score a crosshatch pattern on the surfaces to be joined, and then wet them with slip or water.

1 **Cutting out the shapes**
Cut out paper templates. Place them on a large leatherhard slab of clay and cut around each one with a knife before removing the excess.

2 **Finishing the edges**
Dip your index finger in water and rub the cut edges of the shapes to round them. To incise a border around the rims, hold a pointed tool (such as the end of a paint brush) in line with your index finger. As you run your finger around the edges of the shapes, the tool will automatically make a line.

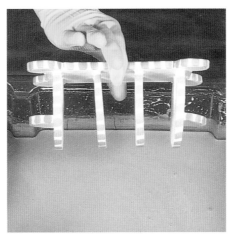

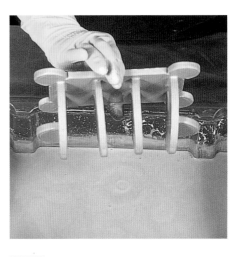

4 Firmly press the shapes together. The joins should now be reinforced by smoothing a thin, soft coil of clay into both sides of the join. When all of the shapes are assembled, blue slip can be brushed on the edges before leaving the piece to slowly dry. Cover the piece lightly with plastic to prevent uneven drying.

5 **Glazing**
After bisque-firing, paint wax on the base of the pot and it is ready to glaze. Be sure its surfaces are dust free, and the glaze is well stirred and of the correct consistency (see p.17). Wearing rubber gloves, hold the toast rack with your index finger and thumb.

6 Dip the piece into the glaze for two seconds, then hold it upside-down over the glaze container until it has stopped dripping. Finally, brush glaze on the bare patches left by your finger and thumb and thoroughly clean all glaze from the base.

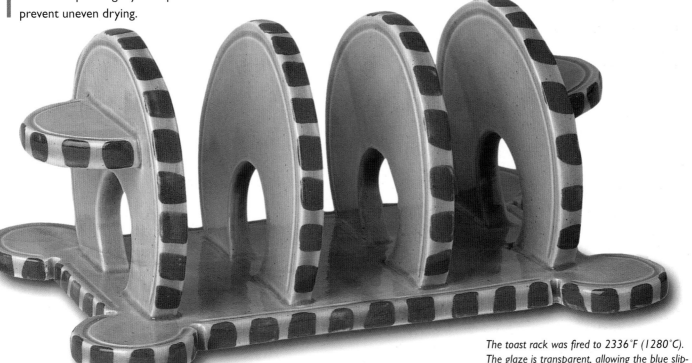

The toast rack was fired to 2336°F (1280°C). The glaze is transparent, allowing the blue slip-brush marks which make the patterned edges to show through. The glaze was colored by adding 2% copper oxide and ¼% cobalt oxide to a transparent base glaze (see pp.16–19). The piece had been bisque (biscuit) fired to 1830°F (1000°C).

MATERIALS

15 lbs. (6.75 kg.) well-prepared white stoneware clay

½ lb. (225 kg.) each of blue, green and yellow colored clay (see p.78)

Cotton cloth for slab rolling (optional)

Paper for templates

Water or slip to join

Blue stoneware glaze for plate and transparent stoneware glaze for the top (see pp.16–19)

TOOLS

Pencil

Scissors

Ruler

Rolling pin

Small hand clay extruder (optional)

Potter's knife

Needle

Brush

EQUIPMENT

Plastic sheets

Wooden boards

Rubber gloves

Firing cones 03 and 7, 8, 9, 10

Kiln

FURTHER INFORMATION

For explanation of unfamiliar words and technical terms, refer to the Glossary on pages 138–141

CHEESE DISH

This project shows the use of colored clay inlay into the slab before the shape is assembled. The clay pattern can be symmetrical or loose and free. If you wish to keep the pattern straight, take care to lightly press the rolling pin over it when rolling the pattern into the slab surface, otherwise it may stretch and distort. With non-rigid patterns this distortion can be used to advantage, as it can greatly enhance the unique effect.

For all domestic ware intended for food use it is important to ensure that all surfaces in contact with the food are smooth and easily cleaned. So spend extra time finishing the inside edges of the base plate and inside the top of the cheese dish, and choose a glaze that will not craze for these surfaces.

As the plate will be glazed on the inside, the top cannot be glaze fired on top of it, so make a bisque-fired flat slab "setter" for the top to sit on during the glaze firing.

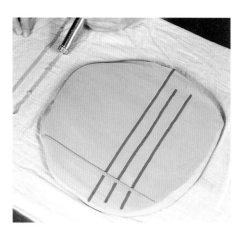

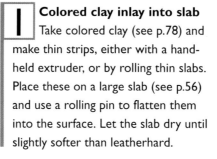

1 Colored clay inlay into slab
Take colored clay (see p.78) and make thin strips, either with a hand-held extruder, or by rolling thin slabs. Place these on a large slab (see p.56) and use a rolling pin to flatten them into the surface. Let the slab dry until slightly softer than leatherhard.

2 Cutting the shapes from a template
Place your paper templates for the walls on the slab, lining them up with the surface pattern as you would in dressmaking, then cut around them. The crest shape for the handle is cut from solid blue clay.

3 **Joining the shapes**
Make strong joins when assembling the walls by scoring a crosshatch pattern on the edges and applying water or slip before pressing the slabs together firmly. Reinforce the insides of the joins by smoothing in a thin, soft coil of clay. Take care to avoid smudging the colored clay pattern when joining the slabs.

4 **Decorative edges**
When all of the walls are joined, cut strips of thin blue clay, score and wet them and join securely on the edges for a decorative border. This will also mask any edges if the colored clay pattern was smudged during assembly. Place the cheese dish top on a leatherhard slab and mark out the shape for the base plate.

5 **Making the base plate**
Score and wet the rim and join on strips of slab to make a thick, wide rim around the plate for the dish to fit into. To ensure a good fit, leave a ³⁄₁₆ in. (5 mm.) gap all around between the dish top and the plate. Turn the plate over on a flat board, and join on four square slabs in the corners as feet which will raise the plate and enable it to be picked up more easily.

6 **Finishing the top**
Score and wet the crest handle and join it on securely. A small wet brush will help you wipe away any slurry from the join. To make the bobbles, roll soft colored clay in your hands, then cut a hole in each one, score and wet both the bobbles and the points on the crest, and join.

After bisque (biscuit) firing to 2012°F (1100°C), the top of the cheese dish was dipped into transparent glaze (see pp.36, 49, 134). The base plate was dipped into a blue glaze (made by adding 2% cobalt oxide to a transparent stoneware glaze – see pp.16–19). They were fired separately 2336°F (1280°C).

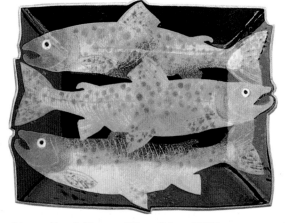

This section explores the making and use of simple one-piece molds. There are two types: "drop-out" molds, which are concave, and "lump" molds, which are convex. The main limitation of these shapes is that they cannot have any undercuts on the form, as this will prevent the clay being released from the mold, even when it has dried and shrunk in size.

The projects are all intended to be press molded, not slip cast. The term press molding describes the process of pressing plastic clay into the mold to make the pot rather than pouring in liquid clay slip. If you have not previously used molds to make ceramic shapes, you will find it helpful to begin by pressing soft clay into ready-made objects before going on to make your own plaster molds. You can use ready-made forms of any rigid material with no undercuts, but if it is less absorbent than plaster, there must be a layer of other material separating the clay from the side of the mold to prevent the clay from sticking to it. Dusting talc

powder over the mold is sometimes sufficient, but shiny surfaces such as glazed ceramic, glass, or metal will require a layer of thin muslin cloth or plastic wrap (cling film) in between the clay and the mold.

Plaster is the most commonly used material for molds made for ceramic manufacture because of its absorbency (it is also relatively inexpensive). The Egyptians used plaster to make pottery 6,000 years ago, and it has continued to be the favored material ever since.

Apart from the project work, it is important to make experimental plaster casts on your own. Begin with a thick slab of soft clay, dusted with talc, then press objects into the slab, remove them (the talc will prevent them from sticking), and make a plaster cast of the patterned slab. Anything from tree bark to pasta will make interesting patterns. These experimental casts will help you to explore the vast potential of textured molds, and will make useful surfaces to roll clay onto for textured or patterned coiled handles or slabs.

Above: Frank Hamer *"Three Salmon." White stoneware, slips brushed over newspaper shapes with additional colors added.*
Top Left: Steve Mattison *"Sky Series." Colored clay, press molded, masking tape resist for glaze then "Raku" fired.*

Chris Speyer
"Cat Plate." White stoneware, press-molded slab, tin glazed with colored glaze stains applied over paper stencil patterns.

Andrea Hylands
"Spiriferidal." Bone china, slip cast and hand-built with airbrushed colored slips, unglazed.

FORMERS AND SIMPLE MOLDS

Gary Bish
Vessel. Press-molded. Wax resist, stencils, and airbrush techniques used to apply underglaze colors and glaze.

Rimas VisGirda
"Champaigne to L.A." Slab-built stoneware coated with thick slip to give cracked surface, to overglaze (on-glaze) enamels applied.

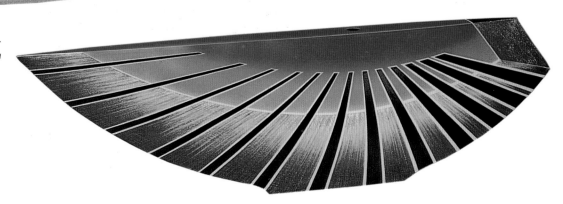

MATERIALS

3 lbs. (1.5 kg.) soft well-prepared clay
(see p.10)

Cardboard tube

Paper

Water or slip for joining

Colored slip for decoration (optional)

Glaze (optional)

TOOLS

Wooden rolling pin

Potter's knife

Needle

Pointed and flat modeling tools

Scissors

EQUIPMENT

Flat board

Kiln and star stilts

Rubber gloves

Firing cones 06 and 03, 02, 01, 1

FURTHER INFORMATION

For explanation of unfamiliar words and
technical terms, refer to the Glossary on
pages 138–141

NAPKIN RINGS

Paper towel tubes can be saved and used as formers. Conveniently, they are just the right size to make napkin rings. Soft clay will stick to the cardboard surface, so it is necessary to wrap paper around it to slide the clay shape off the former.

A paper template is helpful, as this ensures that the clay shape fits the former, as well as enabling you to produce a set of napkin rings of the same shape. To make the template, wrap paper around the tube, allowing a $\frac{5}{16}$ in. (8 mm.) overlap, and cut off the excess (the overlap size corresponds to the size of the mitered cut edges of the clay, as shown in step 2). This strip of paper is your template for cutting the correct length of clay. The edges can be left straight for regular cylinder shapes, or cut to give a shaped edge.

The napkin ring shown here was slip decorated, bisque (biscuit) fired to 1830°F (1000°C) then dipped in transparent glaze and fired supported on a star stilt to 2050°F (1120°C).

3 **Finish the edges**
Cutting slab can leave sharp, unfinished edges, so wet your finger and run it around the cut edges to round them. Take a pointed modeling tool and incise a border line around the shape. Turn the shape over and repeat the process on the reverse side. This border is decorative and therefore optional.

2 **Miter the joins**
Use a potter's knife to cut a 45° angle along one short edge, then carefully pick up the slab, turn it over and repeat the mitered cut on the other end. Score a crosshatch pattern with a needle and wet both of the mitered edges.

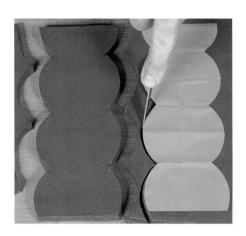

1 **Cut out the shape**
Make a slab approximately ¼ in. (6mm.) thick. Do not allow the slab to dry out as it must be soft to prevent the shapes from cracking. Place your paper template on the surface and cut out the shape.

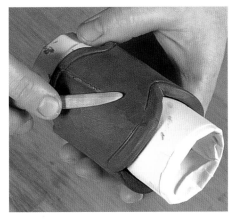

4 Use the former

Wrap a piece of paper around your cardboard tube former (but do not stick it to the tube), and roll the slab shape around the tube. Apply more water or slip to the mitered edges and join them securely.

5 The mitered edges

The mitered ends make a neat join, allowing the surface to be smoothed flat with a modeling tool to completely hide the join line. Mitering produces a larger contact surface for joining, and these joins are therefore stronger than two flat ends butted together. Allow the napkin ring shape to dry to leatherhard.

Latex resist was used to mask out areas when sponging on the yellow and blue slip to make contrasting patterns. Slip-trailed dots were applied to the colored slip surfaces before they dried. After bisque (biscuit) firing to 1830°F (1000°C), they were dipped into transparent glaze and glaze fired on top of metal stilts to 2048°F (1120°C).

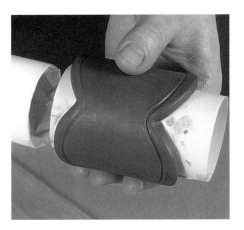

6 Finishing the shape

Slide the paper and napkin ring off the cardboard tube, then peel the paper off. Fill the join line on the inside of the napkin ring with a small soft coil of clay and smooth it into the surface. Slip decoration can now be applied. Dry the napkin ring on its end to prevent the shape from flattening.

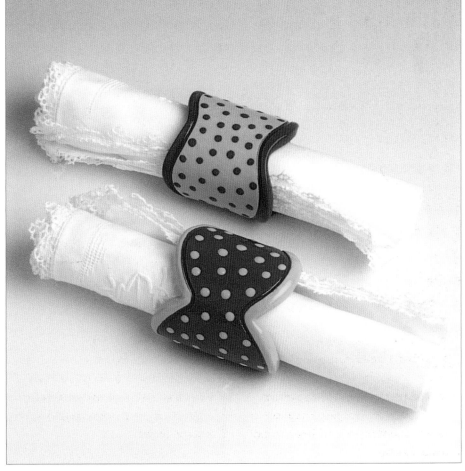

MATERIALS

5 lbs. (2.25 kg.) soft well-prepared
stoneware clay

Cloth to make slab on (optional)

Cylinder former (such as a large soft
drink bottle)

Paper

Water or slip to join

Colored slip to decorate (optional)

Stoneware glaze

TOOLS

Scissors

Rolling pin

Potter's knife

Needle

Brush

Fork

Hole cutter

EQUIPMENT

Flat board

Kiln

Rubber gloves

Firing cones 03 and 7, 8, 9, 10

FURTHER INFORMATION

For explanation of unfamiliar words and
technical terms, refer to the Glossary on
pages 138–141

CUTLERY DRAINER

Recycled household items again come into use for this project. Large plastic soft drink or mineral water bottles are just the right size to make a cutlery drainer large enough to get your hand into to clean it. Use a filled bottle – you can fill a used one with water or use an unopened bottle – as it will hold the shape more rigidly than an empty one.

The cutlery drainer must be raised on added feet for drainage, and will be more stable on three feet than on four. The feet could be made from cut slab, or as shown in this project, from soft coils decorated by pressing a fork into the surface.

After completing the shape it can be slip decorated. The pot shown in this project was banded with dark blue slip (see pp.48 and 114), and when the slip was leatherhard the fork was scored through to reveal the lighter clay color underneath, making a repeat sgraffito pattern. The pot was bisque fired to 2012°F (1100°C), then dipped in transparent stoneware glaze. The glaze was wiped off the base of the feet and then the pot was fired to 2336°F (1280°C).

1 Forming the cylinder
Make a paper template to fit around your former. This shape has a zigzag overlap.

2 Place your paper template on the soft slab and cut around it with a knife. Cut a 45° angle off the straight edge of the slab. This will enable you to make a smooth join inside the cutlery drainer to facilitate cleaning.

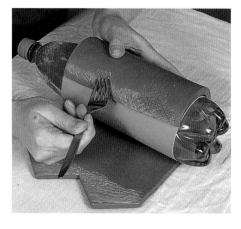

3 Wrap paper around the former to prevent the clay from sticking to it, then roll the slab around it. Mark with a needle where the zigzag touches the other side. Unroll the shape and score a crosshatch pattern, wet it with water or slip and securely join the two sides, retaining the zigzag edge.

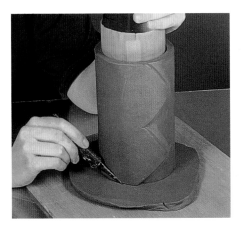

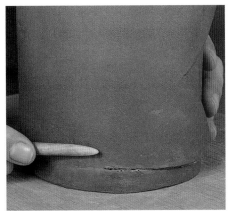

5 Join the edge with your fingers or a modeling tool, and leave to dry to leatherhard before removing the former. Use your finger or a damp brush to smooth over the inside joins. Fill the joins if necessary with coils of soft clay carefully smoothed into the surface. The inside surface must be completely smooth to make the cutlery drainer hygenic.

4 Making the base
Place the cylinder on top of another soft slab of clay and mark around it with a needle, then remove the cylinder and cut out the base with a knife. Score a crosshatch pattern on the edge of the base and on the bottom edge of the cylinder, wet them both with water or slip and securely press together.

6 Adding the feet
Cut and smooth both the inside and outside edges of the drainage holes in the base of the pot before making three feet from soft coils of clay. Here they are patterned by pressing a fork into them. Score and wet the feet and the base of the pot and join securely. Place the pot on plastic to prevent the rim from drying while the feet dry to leatherhard. Use the fork to pattern a length of clay and securely join it onto the top rim.

After bisque (biscuit) firing to 2012°F (1100°C), the pot was dipped into thin transparent glaze and fired to 2336°F (1280°C). The shiny surface of the glaze makes the cutlery drainer easy to clean, and because the glaze is transparent, the blue slip decoration shows through. The stoneware clay fires to a light cream color in an electric kiln, making an effective contrast to the blue slip.

MATERIALS

5 lbs. (2.25 kg.) well-prepared soft white stoneware clay

Muslin cloth

Plastic margarine tub and lid

Transparent stoneware glaze

Blue and yellow over-glaze enamels

Gold luster over-glaze enamel (optional)

Thinners for the enamels and luster

Enamel-printed decal transfer paper (optional)

TOOLS

Scissors

Rolling pin

Potter's knife

Needle

Paint brushes

Wooden butter pat or ruler

Sponge rollers (optional)

EQUIPMENT

Flat board

Banding wheel (optional)

Well ventilated kiln

Kiln props and star stilts

Rubber gloves

Firing cones 03 and 7, 8, 9, 10 plus cones 018, 017, 016 for luster firing

FURTHER INFORMATION

For explanation of unfamiliar words and technical terms, refer to the Glossary on pages 138–141

Water-based over-glaze (on-glaze) colors

BUTTER DISH WITH ENAMEL DECORATION

This project demonstrates two areas of making and decorating: the use of a former to make a lidded pot, and on-glaze enamel decoration. A plastic margarine tub is a good ready-made former for this butter dish, and if you choose an extra large size, it will make a pot big enough to hold a whole regular-sized margarine tub.

White stoneware clay has been chosen to provide a light background for the enamel decoration. Red earthenware clay could be used if given a coating of white slip at the leatherhard stage.

1 Cutting out the shapes
Flatten a plastic tub. Place the shape on a soft slab ³⁄₁₆ in. (5mm.) thick, and cut around it with a knife.

2 Cut out the lid at the same time, so that the pot and the lid will dry together. Place the margarine tub lid on a soft slab ³⁄₁₆ in. (5 mm.) thick and cut around it, allowing an extra ³⁄₈ in. (10 mm.) all around.

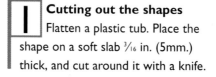

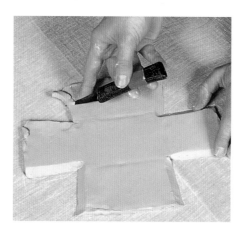

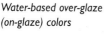

3 Return to the base shape and cut all of the edges at a 45° angle. Score a crosshatch pattern on each, wet with water, then fold the walls up.

ON-GLAZE ENAMELS

Important: Read page 16 before working with enamels.

Unfired enamels and lusters will come off or be marked if they are touched. In step 13, you will see how the lid is supported by kiln props with star stilts on top of them, so that the inside glazed surface of the lid is resting on the stilts. Using this method allows you to pick up the props and lid together to place them in the kiln for firing without touching the lid at all.

4 Pressing the pot into the former

Fold the margarine tub back into its original shape and put tape around the outside to hold the corners in place. Drape butter muslin over it, gently place the clay box into the lined plastic tub, and press in firmly.

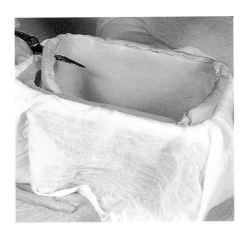

5 Add soft coils of clay in all the corners to reinforce the joins, then carefully smooth down the entire inside surface with your fingers or a rubber scraper. Carefully trim the rim by running a knife along the top edge, using the top of the plastic tub to guide your knife. Smooth down the cut edge to make a rounded rim.

6 Making the lid

Place muslin on the cut-out slab, replace the plastic lid centrally on top and pull the muslin up around it. Fold up the wide rim of the slab around the muslin-wrapped plastic lid, pressing the clay in at the corners, and trim off the excess clay by running a knife along the top edge of the plastic lid. Turn the whole thing over onto plastic.

7 Turning out

Leave both pot and lid supported by their formers for 24 hours, with the top rims covered in plastic wrap to prevent them from drying before the rest of the pot. Then turn the pot out, and remove the muslin-wrapped plastic from the lid. The clay may still be too soft to work on since the plastic formers are non absorbent, so leave to dry until leatherhard.

8 Finishing surfaces

Scrape down the inside and outside surfaces of the pot and lid with a metal scraper to make them flat and smooth. It is essential to have completely smooth surfaces inside to allow the finished butter dish to be easily cleaned.

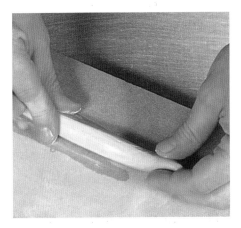

9 Making the knob

The knob is shaped like a curl of butter. Roll a small coil of soft clay, tapering the ends slightly. The coil should be longer than the intended final length to allow for trimming. Wet your index finger and thumb in water, then run them back and forth along the coil to flatten it into a half almond section.

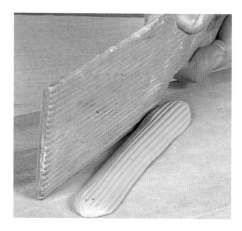

10 When the stretched clay length is dry enough to not be sticky, use a butter pat to press curved lines into the surface. If you do not have a butter pat, use the edge of a ruler to press a series of lines into the surface to give the same pattern.

11 Trim the ends, round them smooth, and roll the clay to make a butter-curl shape. Score the center of the top of the lid and the underside of the knob, wet them and press them firmly together to join. You must support the underside of the lid when pressing on the knob to prevent the lid from distorting.

12 **On-glaze enamel decoration**
After the glaze firing do not touch the pot without gloves or a cloth, as the oils from your skin will prevent the enamels from adhering to the surface of the pot. Mix blue enamel to a milky consistency, and paint each flower with five single brush marks. Having the pot on its side makes the painting easier.

13 When you have completed the blue flowers, apply yellow enamel to the butter-curl knob, and small yellow dots in between the flowers. Finally brush gold enamel onto the edge of the lid. Note that the lid is supported on top of two kiln props so that you can avoid touching it and spoiling the decoration.

Enamels must be applied thinly to avoid bubbling during the firing. Gold luster is particularly sensitive to thickness. Always test fire first. If gold luster is too thin it will fire purple to black in color, but if too thick, it will flake and peel off. The butter dish was bisque (biscuit) fired to 2012°F (1100°C), dipped into transparent glaze, and glaze fired to 2336°F (1280°C), and then the enamels and lusters were fired to 1436°F (780°C).

DECORATING TILES

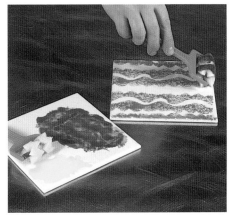

1 **Ready-made blank ware**
Enamel decoration can be applied to glazed surfaces using many of the techniques shown throughout this book. Here the cut-sponge method used for slip printing earlier (see p.58) has been used to print blue enamel onto a tile. The other tile is having sgraffitto decoration scratched through the blue enamel layer.

2 These small house painting sponge rollers were frozen and cut to give a rouletted sponge pattern. Many of the techniques currently popular for furniture or wall decoration in the home, such as stenciling, can be used for on-glaze enamel application.

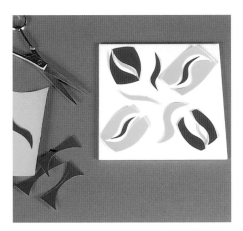

1 **On-glaze enamel transfer paper**
Enamel transfer paper can be bought ready printed in sheets of plain color. These can be applied either to your own glaze-fired work or to ready-made "blank" ware. Cut out the shapes using sharp scissors.

2 Place one shape at a time into lukewarm water. In a few moments the top will slide off of the backing paper. The enamel must be applied top up, and since both sides look the same, it is important to keep the enamel on the paper until you slide it onto the glazed surface.

3 Hold down the edge of the enamel shape with a finger to prevent it sliding. Wrap cotton cloth around your index finger and gently smooth down the surface of the enamel shape. This will push out any trapped air bubbles from underneath the enamel, and dry the surface.

MATERIALS

1 lb. (450 g.) well-prepared soft white stoneware clay

Muslin cloth

Plastic wrap

Round-shaped former

Water or slip for joins

Colored slips and/or underglaze colors to decorate (optional)

Transparent or colored stoneware glaze

TOOLS

Potter's knife

Needle

Thin-edged modeling tool

Paint brushes

Metal scraper

EQUIPMENT

Banding wheel

Kiln

Rubber gloves

Firing cones 03 and 02, 01, 1

FURTHER INFORMATION

For explanation of unfamiliar words and technical terms, refer to the Glossary on pages 138–141

PERFUME BOTTLE

This project explores the joining of multiple shapes taken from the same former, and adding a hand modeled stopper. When choosing a ready-made former, be sure that it has a simple "drop-out" shape – that is, a form with no undercuts which would trap the clay and prevent it from dropping out when the mold is turned upside-down.

Joining two bowls together at the rim is a very useful basic forming technique. It traps the air inside, making the shape much stronger and more durable. For this bottle, the rims are cut into V shapes which fit together. This doubles the surface area and will give a stronger join than two flat-topped rims.

As the pot dries it shrinks, but the volume of air trapped inside stays the same. This creates internal pressure, pushing the wall out, and if you do not puncture the form before the pot dries past the leatherhard stage, this pressurised air can cause any weak spots such as joins to crack open. Pots with trapped air are also more likely to blow out during kiln firing.

1 **Press the shapes**
Make a pinch pot slightly larger than the inside shape of your former. Place plastic wrap over the bowl shapes of the former, and press the soft pinch pot into the former.

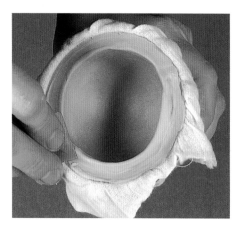

2 Use a knife to trim off the excess clay at the top of the bowl shape to make a flat rim. While turning the pot in its former around in your hand, make a "V" shaped indent around the top rim by pressing a wedge-shaped tool as you rotate the pot. Here a piece of cut plastic is used.

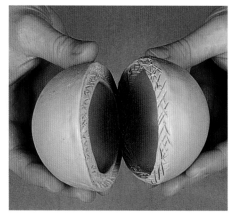

3 **Joining the shapes**
Remove the first bowl from the former and repeat steps 1 and 2, except for the final shape of the top rim. This time carefully pinch the top rim into an upside down V shape. Score a crosshatch pattern on the rims, wet with water or slip, and join the rims together securely without denting the form.

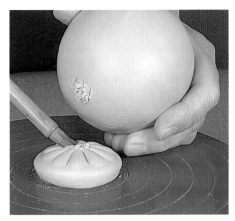

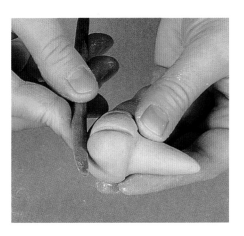

4 Making the stem foot

This former has a relief-patterned base which the clay will pick up well when pressed into it. If you are using a plain bowl shape as your former you can make the stem foot by pressing a shallower bowl shape from the same former. Always cover non-porous formers with plastic wrap or muslin to prevent the clay from sticking.

5

When the sphere shape is leatherhard scrape down the surface with a metal scraper to smooth it. Fill in any unevenness on the join line with soft clay and smooth over. Also trim and give a rounded, smooth finish to the edge of the stem foot. Score and wet the stem foot center and the bottom of the sphere shape and securely join together.

6 Making the stopper

Hand model the stopper from solid clay. Begin by tapering one end to a point, keeping the other end spherical. Press a thin-edged modeling tool into the soft clay to form segments like an orange, and then cut a small round hole in the top of the pot to fit the stopper.

When leatherhard, the bottle was decorated with slip and underglaze colors using paper and latex resist, brushing and slip trailing (see pp.44, 52, 53, 58, 87, 114). After bisque (biscuit) firing to 2012°F (1100°C) the pot was glazed with a transparent glaze and the foot ring was sponged clean. The stopper was dipped into the glaze and placed on a metal stilt during the glaze firing at 2084°F (1140°C),

MATERIALS

Ready-made shape to mold (optional)

Clay for making model

1 lb. 13 oz. (775 g.) dry plaster powder

¼ cup water for joining

4 oz. (115 g.) of each colored clay—
green, blue, light blue, yellow

Blue slip for joining the agate shapes

Plastic wrap

Plastic sheets

Paper for template

TOOLS

Linoleum for "cottle"

Metal clip

String

Jug

Surform scraper

Rigid metal kidney scraper

Rolling pin

Very thin cutting wire

Needle

Brush

Potter's knife

Scissors

Flexible metal scraper

Steel (wire) wool (optional)

EQUIPMENT

Board

Drying cupboard (optional)

Face mask with dust filters

Rubber gloves (if using steel wool)

Kiln

Firing cones 06 and 03, 02, 01, 1

FURTHER INFORMATION

For explanation of unfamiliar words and
technical terms, refer to the Glossary on
pages 138–141

COLORED-CLAY BOWL

This project introduces two new areas: making simple "drop-out" molds from plaster, and making colored clay. It is essential that the form used to make a drop-out mold has no undercuts. As with the ready-made mold shapes used previously in projects (see pages 70 and 74), the pot must literally drop out when the mold is turned upside down, and any undercuts, such as a curved-in rim, would hold the clay in the mold, making it impossible to remove.

Before making a colored-clay bowl, it is advisable to first produce a single-colored one. A very effective method of creating an interesting pattern on the outside surface is to place coils or round balls of soft clay in the mold, then smooth over the inside surface to join the pieces together. This will produce a pattern of shallow grooves on the outside surface, between each of the coils or ball shapes. (See the final picture for the decorative letters project.)

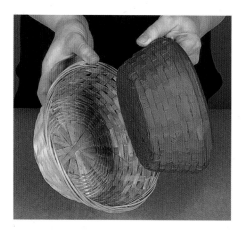

Textured ready-made molds
You can choose drop-out molds with a ready-made surface pattern which will be repeated on the clay. A large pinch pot was pressed into this basket and the inside surface smoothed down with a rubber scraper. The bowl had shrunk when it dried to leatherhard, and the bowl was easily released from the basket.

Shapes for molding
You can make plaster molds from plastic containers (providing they have no undercuts). The flat base of this plastic bowl has been rounded by smoothing soft clay over it. The rim must be sealed to the board to prevent plaster from seeping underneath, and the board must then be oiled to prevent the plaster from sticking to it. Follow steps 2–8 to complete the mold.

1 You can also throw your own shapes to cast in plaster (see section on Throwing and Turning). Attach a throwing bat to the wheel and center a solid lump of clay, then smooth the surface. If you use a varnished wooden bat, it does not need to be oiled. Cut a strip of linoleum to make a "cottle" around the lump.

2 **"Cottling-up"**
A metal clip will hold the linoleum in place while you tie string tightly around it. Make a loop on one end of the string, then feed the other end through the loop and pull tightly before tying a strong knot to secure.

3 Press soft coils of clay all around the base of the cottle and smooth over the surface to make a watertight seal. Warning: if the clay has not made a proper seal the plaster will leak out of the base of the cottle when you pour plaster into the mold.

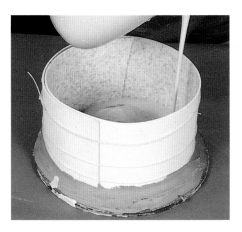

4 **Pouring in plaster**
Mix 1 lb. 13 oz. (775 g.) of plaster with 1 pint (575 ml.) of water (see pp. 20 and 21). Pour it into a good pouring jug and then into your mold. Hold the jug in one spot as you pour the plaster to prevent splashing and the formation of air bubbles. Continue pouring until the plaster covers the clay shape by the same thickness as the walls.

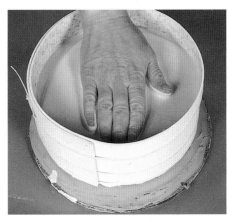

5 Place your hand on the surface of the plaster and gently move it up and down to bring any air bubbles to the surface. Quickly empty any excess plaster from your bucket and jug into a plastic bag or cardboard box—**never down the sink!**

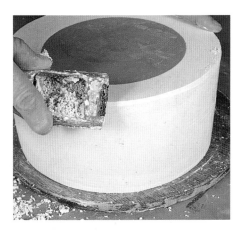

6 **Clean up the mold**
When the plaster has set hard, take off the cottle, and then use a Surform blade and/or rigid metal scraper to remove sharp edges and any plaster that might chip off and contaminate your clay work. Remove the original clay shape from the mold taking care not to scrape the surface of the plaster. Dry the mold (see p. 79).

COLORED CLAY

To make colored clay, pour ³/₁₆ in. (5 mm.) layer of colored slip (see p.14) onto flat, clean, dry plaster. Within minutes the plaster will have absorbed enough moisture from the slip to make it workable clay. Wrap the colored clay in plastic to prevent it from drying further. Be very careful not to contaminate one color with another.

7 **Colored clay**
Roll very thin slabs of colored clay between sheets of plastic to prevent the clay from sticking. Lightly spraying the sheets with water first will help prevent the clay from sticking. Thin slabs dry very quickly so always keep them covered with plastic.

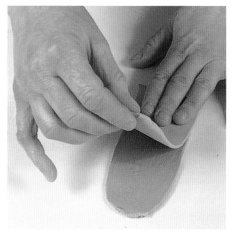

8 Brush colored slip on the top of one slab and then place a different colored slab on top. To prevent trapping air bubbles between the layers, press the slabs on from one end, pressing the clay down until it reaches the other end, as shown here.

9 When you have joined all the layers together, cut them in half, brush on colored slip and join the two halves together to make the shape half the length and twice the thickness. Lightly roll the layered clay to strengthen the joins between the layers and slightly stretch the slab.

10 Use a very fine wire or fishing line to make ³/₁₆ in. (5 mm.) thick slices of the multicolored layers, and keep these wrapped in plastic to prevent them from drying.

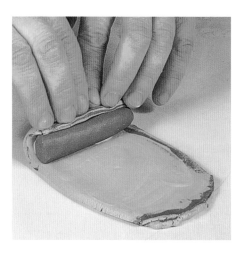

11 Another variation is to make a coil of colored clay and then roll a slab of layered colors around it. If you do not wish to join the coil to the slab surface with colored slip then brush water onto the top surface of the slab and roll it around the coil.

DRYING PLASTER MOLDS

Plaster is the most commonly used material for making molds for ceramic production because of its absorbency when dry. It is important to dry your newly made molds before use. Plaster, however, will become soft and unusable if overheated or too dry. New molds will dry in a warm room over the period of a week or two, depending on humidity, but you can force-dry them in a drying cupboard where hot air is circulated. You can make a drying cupboard by cutting a hole at the base of an old wardrobe, placing an electric fan heater up to the hole so that the heat is directed into the wardrobe, then cutting ventilation holes at the top of the wardrobe.
(Never allow electrical appliances to overheat or cause a hazard.)
Alternatively, an electric fan oven on its lowest setting and with the door ajar will work, but bear in mind that humidity will be created during the drying. The drying temperature should not exceed 136°F (40°C).
Small molds should be dry enough to use within a day or two of this forced drying. Molds can also be dried on top of your kiln if propped up on stilts to raise them off the hot surface, or placed on top of radiators to dry. Do not over dry the mold. As soon as it feels dry, it is ready to use.

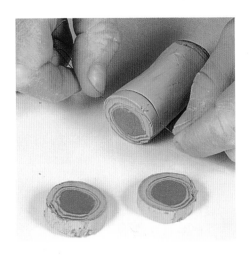

12 Again, use a fine wire to cut ³⁄₁₆ in. (5 mm.) slices off the layered coil shape and keep them wrapped in plastic to keep them soft.

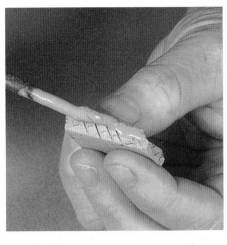

13 **Press molding with colored clay**
When you have made enough clay slices to fill the mold, score and wet the edges of the layered slices with water or colored slip before pressing them into the mold.

14 Press them and try to fill the entire mold quickly to prevent the first pieces drying before the rest. The layered slices can be interspersed with single-color ones to break up the pattern. Here yellow clay slab is joined in between the multicolored slab. You can make up the pattern as you fill the mold.

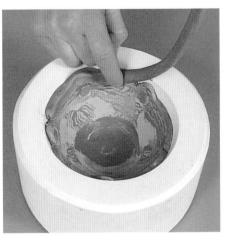

15 To give the bowl a single-colored rim, score the top edge of the clay in the mold and wet it with water or slip. Place on a long thin slab length and join it securely to the lower layer of clay. Press the entire surface firmly with your fingers in order to "tension" the clay (see p.10), then smooth it with a scraper.

16 **Removing the pot from the mold**
Do not try to force the bowl out of the mold. When it has dried to leatherhard, place your hand or a wooden board over the mold opening, pick up the mold and turn it over. The leatherhard pot will have shrunk and will drop out of the mold onto your hand or wooden board.

17 **Revealing the pattern**
The surface pattern will be smudgy when the pot comes out of the mold, but at the leatherhard stage it can be scraped with a metal scraper to reveal the crisp pattern. Always wear a face mask with a dust filter when dealing with dry clay dust, and dispose of the scrapings carefully to prevent them from contaminating other clay work or from posing a health hazard.

18 **Template for scalloped edge**
Wrap a strip of paper around the rim of the bowl, cut it to fit the diameter exactly, then place the two ends together and fold the strip in half repeatedly. Draw a semi-circle with a compass and cut through all thicknesses of the paper, then open out the template, replace it and mark the cutting lines.

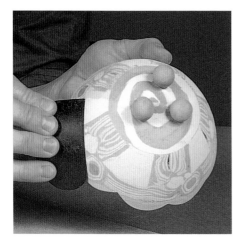

19 **Finishing the bowl**
After cutting the scalloped rim and rounding the cut edges with a wet finger, make three round balls of soft clay. Score and wet these and the bottom of the bowl where they are to be joined, and fix in position. When the pot has dried completely, put on your face mask with dust filter and carefully scrape back the final surface. Steel wool works well for this but do wear protective gloves.

After bisque (biscuit) firing to 1830°F (1000°C), the bowl was dipped into transparent earthenware glaze (see pp.16–19, 115) and fired on top of metal stilts (see p.24). A 2084°F (1120°C) glaze was chosen to give brighter color. The pot could have been left unglazed, or glazed only on the inside.

NUMBERS AND LETTERS

The number and letter patterns used to make these molds can be traced from books or magazines or can be cut out of newspapers. Computers could also be used to print out the typeface and size of your choice. Press-molded decorative numbers or letters can be used in many ways. If removed from the molds before they become drier than leatherhard, you can join separate ones to the sides of pots to make commemorative work (using the same method as the sprig molds shown on page 128), or they could be made into name plates for interior doors, such as bedrooms and bathrooms. The number plaque shown in this project could either be a house number or made into a ceramic birthday card for someone special. If intended for outdoor use, follow the frost-proofing advice on page 56. Note also the information on page 59 on how to avoid warping on flat tile shapes.

MATERIALS

Thick "exhibition" matt board or thick cardboard

Clay for making model

1 lb. 13 oz. (775 g.) dry plaster powder and 1 pint (575 ml.) water to mix for each mold

4 lbs. (1.8 kg.) well-prepared white stoneware clay

4 oz. (115 g.) each of colored clay: green, blue, yellow

Plastic wrap and plastic sheets

Tracing paper for template

TOOLS

Adjustable wooden mold frame

String

Jug

Surform scraper

Rigid metal kidney scraper

Rolling pin

Needle

Brush

Potter's knife

Small hand clay extruder (optional)

EQUIPMENT

Board

Drying cupboard (optional)

Kiln

Rubber gloves

Firing cones 03 and 7, 8, 9, 10

FURTHER INFORMATION

For explanation of unfamiliar words and technical terms, refer to the Glossary on pages 138–141

Tracing paper, potter's knife, ready-made transparent glaze powder

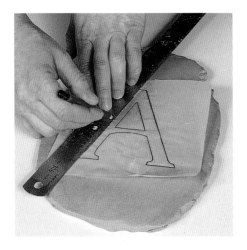

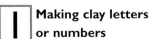

1 **Making clay letters or numbers**
Draw your letters or numbers on the surface of a ⅜ in. (1 cm.) slab by pressing lightly with a pointed modeling tool or pencil around the outline of the shape. This will leave an indented mark on the clay's surface.

2 Use a potter's knife to cut out the shapes. Note that the knife blade can cut at an angle to make a sloping edge, which not only looks nice but also ensures that the edges will have no undercuts. Remove excess clay from the letter shape, then round off the cut edges with a wet finger.

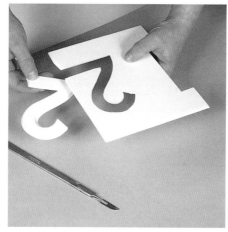

3 Plaster casting
Place the clay letters on a flat, smooth surface such as formica. Set up adjustable wall cottle boards around the shape, leaving a minimum 1⅜ in. (3 cm.) gap between the wall and the letter. To make the plaster cast, follow steps 4–6 on page 77.

4 Making cardboard letters or numbers
You can also make the shapes out of cardboard. Trace them (or draw freehand) onto exhibition matt board or thick cardboard, then cut them out with a sharp scalpel or craft knife— taking extra care not to cut yourself. As with all other drop-out molds there must be no undercuts on the shapes to be molded.

5 Use glue or double-sided adhesive tape to attach the cardboard numbers on top of another square of cardboard, use double-sided tape to secure this to a flat, smooth-topped surface and follow steps 4–6 on page 77.

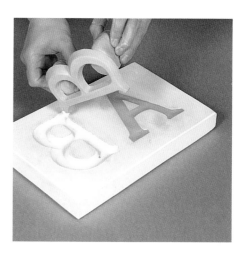

6 Finishing the molds
When the plaster has set, scrape any rough plaster off of the molds and round any sharp edges with a Surform blade or metal scraper. Remove the original clay forms from the molds and dry them as explained on page 79.

7 Press-molding the shapes
Press a smooth surfaced lump of clay into the mold, working it in from one end to the other to prevent trapping air bubbles. Now scrape back the excess clay with a metal scraper, taking care not to scrape the plaster mold. Smooth the surface of the clay with a wet rubber scraper.

8 These thin clay shapes will be dried within minutes. As soon as the edges of the clay have come away from the sides of the mold, take two pieces of soft clay and press them onto the clay letter. This will stick to the dry clay, allowing you to lift the shape out of the mold.

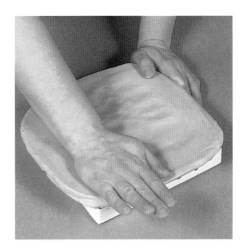

9 Press-molding a number plaque

Press yellow stained clay into the numbers and clean away excess clay from the mold, as in step 7. Score a crosshatch pattern into the surface of the yellow clay with a needle.

10 Make a patterned slab by rolling colored clay shapes into the surface of a soft slab of clay, as shown on page 62. Wet the scored marks on the yellow clay numbers with water before pressing the decorated slab on top. Press the slab onto the mold from one corner out to the opposite edges to avoid trapping air bubbles.

11 Firmly press the slab onto the mold using the flat of your hand. Now use a rolling pin to flatten and smooth the surface. Trim the excess clay off the edges of the mold by carefully running a potter's knife along the edge as shown on page 87.

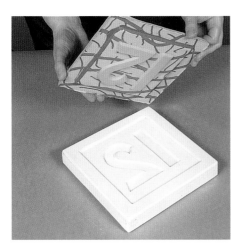

12 When the clay has dried to leatherhard, it can be removed from the mold, which should then be cleaned with a damp sponge and left to dry. Trim the edges of the clay plaque and round the cut edges with a wet finger. Cut holes to allow the plaque to be hung on a wall.

After bisque (biscuit) firing to 2012°F (1100°C), the backs were waxed. The letter plaque was dipped into the same glaze as used for the Monster Money Box (see p.34). The number plaque was dipped into transparent glaze. After sponging the glaze off the backs, they were fired to 2336°F (1280°C).

MATERIALS

6 to 16 lbs. (2.7 to 7.2 kg.) clay for making model

10 lbs. 14 oz. (4.85 kg.) dry plaster powder and 6 pints (96 fl. oz.) water to mix

6 lbs. (2.7 kg.) well-prepared white stoneware clay

4 lbs. (1.8 kg.) well-prepared black colored clay

Plastic sheets

Colored slip to band top edge

TOOLS

Linoleum for cottle

String

Jug

Surform scraper

Rigid metal scraper

Rolling pin

Needle

Brush

Potter's knife

Cutting wire

EQUIPMENT

Board

Drying cupboard (optional)

Kiln

Rubber gloves

Face mask with filter

Firing cones 03 and 7, 8, 9, 10

FURTHER INFORMATION

For explanation of unfamiliar words and technical terms, refer to the Glossary on pages 138–141

Rubber scraper and Chinese brush

MARBLED OVAL BOWL

This project deals first with making the walls of a large mold of even thickness; second, with making an oval shape from a round bowl, and third, with making marbled slabs. The initial round bowl shape was made by throwing and turning a bowl and placing it upside-down, but if you are unable to throw and turn, you can make the shape from solid clay. Begin by making a template of the round bowl's external shape from stiff cardboard or wood, then press a solid lump of very soft clay with your hands, making it as close as possible to the shape of the upside-down bowl. Now move the template over the shape, scraping off any high lumps, and filling in any hollows with soft clay. Continue scraping the template over the solid clay until it is the desired shape and has an even, smooth surface. This is the same process as "sledging," shown on page 93, but uses clay instead of plaster. Now follow the 18 steps of the project.

If the colors of the marbled clay smear while you're scraping, stop and let it dry more before proceeding.

Be careful when working with dry, unfired clay, as it is extremely brittle, and even the slightest knock will cause cracking.

1 Making the clay form
Make a clay form in the shape of a round upside-down bowl. Measure the center point of the base, draw a line down the middle. Measure ¾ in. (2 cm.) away from the center line on each side of it. Use a straight piece of linoleum as a guide for cutting lines.

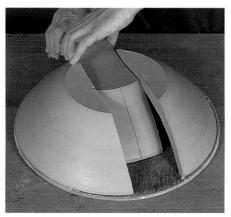

2 Cut the 1½ in. (4 cm.) width out of the form and remove this excess clay.

3 Score a crosshatch pattern onto both edges of the form, wet with water or slip, then press the two sides together. Join a coil of soft clay into the joined edge and smooth over with a metal scraper.

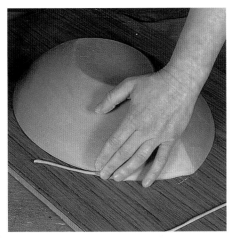

4 Place a thin coil of soft clay all around the bottom edge of the form and smooth it down. This will seal the hollow form onto the surface, preventing plaster from seeping underneath, and also ensure that the bottom edge of the form has no undercut on the mold.

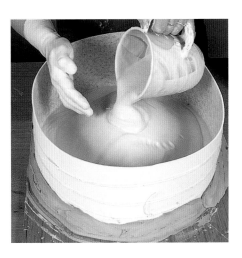

5 **Casting the form in plaster**
After securely cottling-up the form (see p.77), mix 10 lbs. 14 oz. (4.85 kg.) dry plaster powder with 6 pints (96 fl. oz.) water as shown on pages 20–21. Pour one jugfull at a time onto the top of the shape. Maintain a steady stream to avoid splashes and air bubbles.

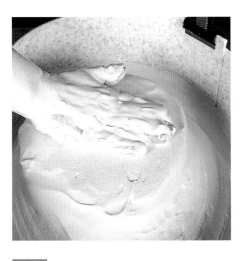

6 Before the plaster sets, scoop it up toward the top as evenly as possible. The mold should be 1³⁄₁₆ to 1⁹⁄₁₆ in. (3 to 4 cm.) thick for its entire section. Avoid making thick and thin sections, as this would cause the mold to dry pots unevenly.

7 After the plaster has set, remove the cottle and clean up the rough surface of the mold by scraping it with a stiff metal scraper. Once again try to make the surfaces as even as possible. If there are any deep hollows, score their surface, mix more plaster and fill them before scraping back.

8 Turn the mold over and continue to scrape away rough edges and sharp corners. The entire surface of the plaster mold must be smooth with rounded edges, to prevent plaster from chipping off and contaminating clay work. Remove the clay former and dry the mold (see p.79).

9 **Making marbled clay**
Make ³⁄₁₆ in. (5 mm.) thick slabs and cut them into rectangles of approximately 12 x 4½ in. (30 x 12 cm.). Make four rectangles of soft white clay and three of black colored clay (see p.78). Press the slabs together in alternating colored layers (see p.78).

10 Slice the layered clay in half lengthwise with a cutting wire. Fold each in half, and place one on top of the other with the curved ends of each folded slab at opposite ends.

11 Knead the clay (see p.11), making only two or three turns at most to marble the colors together. Be careful not to knead too much, as this will make the pattern lose its clarity and become muddy.

12 Press the marbled lump of clay into a thick, flat cube shape with your hands, cut through the width to make two thick slabs, then join the edges of the two slabs together and roll them into one large slab ³⁄₁₆ in. (5 mm.) thick (see p.56).

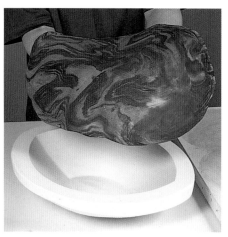

13 **Pressing the clay into the mold**
Lift up the slab, either supporting its weight with your arms to avoid tearing the edge, or using a cloth or plastic sheet to lift it. Place the slab centrally on top of the mold and gently press it down into the shape.

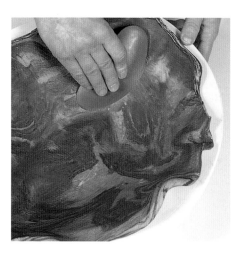

14 Do not allow the top edge of the slab to fold over, as folds can cause cracks in the clay as it dries out. Use a rubber scraper to press the slab firmly into the mold. Do not worry about smudging the surface pattern as this will be scraped back later.

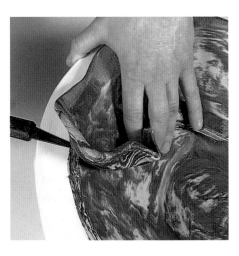

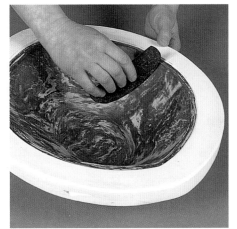

| 15 | **Trimming the rim**
The undulating rim can be retained, but if you want a straight rim, trim it off by running a knife along the top edge of the plaster mold, then round the cut edge with a wet finger or template and leave the bowl to dry.

| 16 | **Finishing the surface**
When the bowl is a little drier than leatherhard, scrape back the surface with a metal scraper. Place a flat ware board over the mold, turn over the mold and remove it, leaving the bowl upside-down on the ware board. See picture 16 on page 95 for how to turn the bowl right side up.

| 17 | Paint colored slip onto the top rim, using the same slip that made the colored clay. The slip does not need to be applied accurately, as any drips or splotches will be scraped away.

After bisque (biscuit) firing to 2012°F (1100°C), the salad bowl was glazed inside only with a transparent stoneware glaze. A damp sponge was used to wipe any excess glaze off of the outside of the pot. It was fired to 2336°F (1280°C), then the unglazed outside of the bowl was polished with fine wet and dry sandpaper.

| 18 | Put on a face mask with a suitable dust filter attached. Use a metal scraper or steel wool to scrape down and finish the surface. (Wear protective gloves if using steel wool.) This final scraping back will reveal the crisp pattern of the marbling.

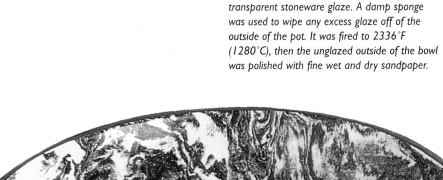

MATERIALS

Suitably sized plastic container

7 lbs. 4 oz. (3.26 kg.) dry plaster powder and 4 pints (64 fl. oz.) water to mix

2 lbs. (900 g.) soft clay

3 lbs. 10 oz. (1.65 kg.) dry plaster powder and 2 pints (32 fl. oz.) water (for stem foot of mold)

Tracing paper

7 lbs. (3.15 kg.) well-prepared white stoneware clay

Plastic sheets

TOOLS

Jug

Surform scraper

Rigid metal kidney scraper

Tracing paper and pencil

Forged-steel rounded tip tool for incised pattern

Rolling pin

Needle

Brush

Potter's knife

EQUIPMENT

Flat boards

Drying cupboard (optional)

Banding wheel

Kiln

Rubber gloves

Firing cones 03 and 7, 8, 9, 10

FURTHER INFORMATION

For explanation of unfamiliar words and technical terms, refer to the Glossary on pages 138–141

HORS D'OEUVRE TRAY

A "lump" mold is made for this project. This is a one-piece mold in which the clay is pressed over a convex shape, rather than into a concave shape as in a "drop-out" mold. Lump molds can be produced from clay shapes or ready-made objects; in this project a plastic container has been used for the form. The former must not have any undercuts on the shape or the set plaster will not release from it—even the smallest bump on the inside rim of the former will hold the plaster in with no hope of release.

The lump mold for the tray could be made by the same process shown for the dish in the following project.

Plaster molds can have added pattern or texture. By incising into the plaster molds you can produce anything from detailed and meticulous compositions to rough abstract textures. Patterns and textures can also be applied to the formers prior to casting the mold. For example, thin clay strips could be attached to the inside of the plastic former in this project before the plaster is poured in.

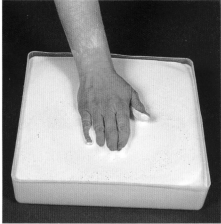

1   Making the lump mold Mix 7 lbs. 4 oz. (3.26 kg.) of dry plaster powder with 4 pints (64 fl. oz.) of water as shown on pages 20–21. Pour the plaster into the clean plastic container right up to the top. Put any excess plaster into a plastic bag to be thrown away.

2 Put your hand on the surface and gently move the wet plaster up and down to agitate the surface and thus release air bubbles. To avoid skin irritation, wear rubber gloves when touching plaster.

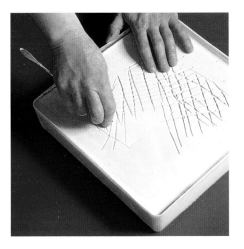

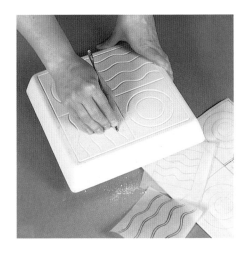

3 **Making the stem foot**
As soon as the plaster has set, score deep marks into the surface in a crosshatch pattern. These score marks help create a strong bond between the base of the mold and the raised stem foot that will be added to the middle of the shape.

4 Make a 1½ in. (4 cm.) high, watertight wall of soft clay around the score marks. Flare the clay walls out at the top rim to give the stem foot an overhang which will make the mold much easier to pick up when it is upside down. Mix 3 lb. 10 oz. (1.65 kg.) dry plaster with 2 pints (32 fl. oz.) water and pour into the stem foot.

5 **Incising pattern**
After removing the mold from the plastic container and cleaning it up by scraping off any rough or sharp edges, turn it over to reveal the flat smooth top surface. This can have a pattern traced onto it and then incised into it by scraping a round-ended forged steel tool across the surface. Keep the tracing-paper pattern to use for the dishes in the following project.

ALTERNATIVE PROCESS

If you cannot find a ready-made shape for the tray, use the following traditional method of making lump molds. Begin by making a solid lump of clay in the shape of the upside-down tray. Follow the steps shown in this project to make a plaster "drop-out" mold, then apply continuous coats of "soft soap" to its upper surface, working it in with a sponge to produce a lather which is wiped away. Repeat this process until a drop of water will bead off the surface of the plaster rather than sinking in. Then follow the steps on pages 88 and 89 to make the mold.

Beware: The plaster will not release from the former if insufficient soft soap layers are applied. An alternative to using soft soap is to press a thin slab of clay into the drop-out mold, covering the entire surface including the rim. The clay will prevent the plaster shapes sticking together, and can be smooth or have an added pattern.

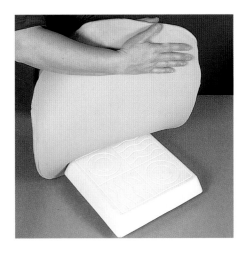

6 **Press molding the tray**
When the mold has dried (see p.79), make a ¼ in. (6 mm.) thick slab from 6 lbs. (2.7 kg.) of the soft, well-prepared clay. Pick the slab up, supporting it with your hands and arms to prevent the edge from tearing, and place it centrally onto the mold. Use a piece of cloth or plastic sheet to move large slabs of soft clay.

7 Press the surface firmly with the flat of your hand, working from one corner out. This will push out any trapped air bubbles as well as ensure that the clay has completely filled the incised pattern.

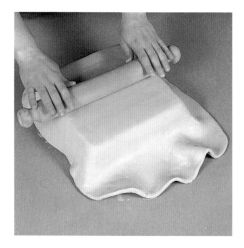

8 Press the clay up to the corners of the shape. Use a rolling pin to flatten the top surface as well as the sides. Smooth the entire surface with a rubber scraper. Trim off the excess clay by running a knife along the bottom edge of the mold (see p.95). Round the cut edge by smoothing over it with a wet finger or plastic template.

9 Removing the tray from the mold
As soon as the tray has dried enough to release from the plaster, lift it off the mold. The main danger with using lump molds is that as clay dries it shrinks, but if it is drying over a rigid shape like a lump mold, it will not be able to shrink, so if not removed soon enough the pot will crack.

10 Making the handles
Make a slab of soft clay ¼ in. (6 mm.) thick from the remaining 1 lb. (450 g.) of clay and press it into a portion of the incised pattern on the surface of the lump mold. Allow the slab to dry on the mold to leatherhard.

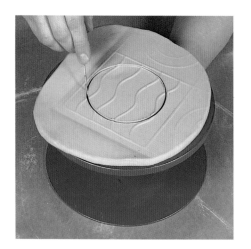

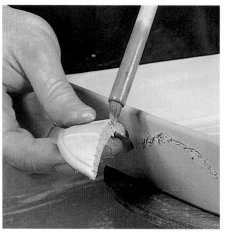

11 Place the patterned slab centrally on a banding wheel or throwing wheel, and use a needle or knife to cut into the soft slab to make a circle while spinning it around. Remove the excess clay around the circle. Smooth down the cut edge with a wet finger or template, and incise a line around the perimeter to make a border edge.

12 Cut the slab in half. Then cut equal lengths off the wide ends to make the desired size for the handles. Gently curve the flat slabs then score and wet the edges of the handles and the place where they are to join onto the tray.

13 Joining on the handles
Firmly press the handles onto the tray to make a secure join, supporting the inside wall of the tray with one hand to prevent distorting the shape of the wall. Any excess soft clay around the join line can be wiped away with a wet brush.

14 Finishing and drying

Place a flat board on top of the tray so that it is sandwiched between two flat boards. Place one hand on the top board and the other hand on the bottom one, turn the tray over and remove the board to expose the base of the tray.

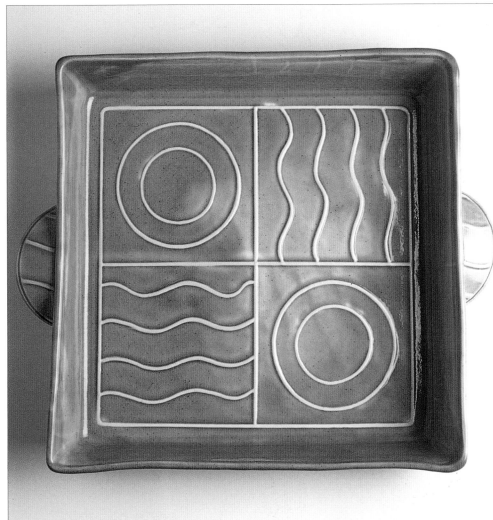

After bisque (biscuit) firing to 2012°F (1100°C), the base was waxed, and the tray was glazed by pouring transparent green stoneware glaze into and over the outside surfaces (see p.49). The glaze was made by adding 2% copper oxide and ½% cobalt oxide to a ready-made transparent glaze and fired to 2336°F (1280°C – see pp.16–19).

15

The pot will dry more evenly upside-down, and this also gives you access to the underside of the handles. Reinforce the joins by pressing on a soft coil of clay and smoothing it into the surface. Cover the entire pot with sheets of dry newspaper to make the drying process slow and even.

MATERIALS

Flat wood or Plexiglas for base

Flat wood or Plexiglas for template

1 lb. 13 oz. (825 g.) dry plaster powder and 1 pint (16 fl. oz.) water to mix

2 lbs. (900 g.) soft clay

4 oz. (115 g.) each colored clay – blue and green

Tracing paper (use the tracing pattern from the previous project)

Plastic sheets

EQUIPMENT

Surform scraper

Rigid metal kidney scraper

Rolling pin

Brush

Potter's knife

"Wet and dry" sandpaper

TOOLS

Flat boards

Jug

Plastic buckets

Rubber gloves

Drying cupboard (optional)

Kiln

Firing cones 03 and 7, 8, 9, 10

FURTHER INFORMATION

For explanation of unfamiliar words and technical terms, refer to the Glossary on pages 138–141

Dry plaster powder and scraper

HORS D'OEUVRE DISHES

"Sledging" is a technique traditionally used to make decorative plaster moldings for ceilings, but it is also well suited to mold-making for ceramics. This method can also be used for making solid clay shapes to use as forms which can then be cast in plaster. The clay form for the fruit bowl drop-out mold, shown on page 84, could have been made by sledging a template over solid soft clay.

Rather than having incised pattern, this project shows how thin slabs of colored clay can be used to make bold patterns on the surface of the pot. The dishes are intended to coordinate with the tray in the previous project, with the colored clay patterns echoing the incised pattern on the tray.

As with all other techniques, it is important to experiment. Apply colored clay on the mold in different ways, using thin slab shapes, hand rolled or extruded lengths or small dots of clay which can make separate shapes or overlap each other. The pattern-making potential is unlimited.

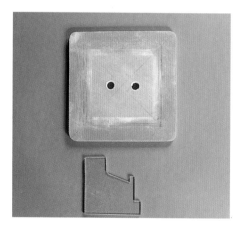

1 Sledging templates
Cut a template from wood or Plexiglas for the walls and top edge of the dish shape using a coping saw, then round the edges with a file and sand them smooth. Make a square wooden base with rounded edges. The size of this square will determine the length of the lump mold sides. Drill two holes in the base. These will fill with plaster and hold the shape in place.

2 The template must have a straight piece cut out from its base which is the same height as the thickness of the base. This makes a lip overhanging the edge which enables the template to follow the outside shape of the base. The shape of the template follows the flat of the base further in than the main wall shape above, to make an undercut under the walls of the mold to create the stem foot.

3 | Sledging the lump mold shape

Mix 1 lb. 13 oz. (825 g.) dry plaster powder with 1 pint (16 fl. oz.) water as shown on pages 20–21. When the plaster becomes thick enough to hold its shape, pour it onto the base. It is advisable to wear rubber gloves to protect your skin.

4

Now it is a race against time, because the plaster sets fast. Before this happens, run the template along all edges of the base to scoop away the excess plaster from the sides, thus beginning to shape the walls of the mold.

5

Keep moving the template around the base, pushing it up against the edge of the base to remove the excess plaster from the sides. Turn the base around to give easier access to all sides as you pull the template around.

6

Put fresh plaster on top to fill in the shape, then continue to pull the template around the base to form the walls of the mold.

7

All four walls must be formed before the plaster sets. Scraping around with the template as the plaster becomes "cheesy" will leave the walls rough, and there will be excess plaster on the top of the mold which will need to be scraped down.

8 | Cleaning up the surfaces

After washing the plaster off of your gloves or hands (in a bucket—not in the sink), dispose of the excess plaster in a bin. When the plaster has set, it is ready to have its surfaces scraped down with a Surform. Remove the rough surface on the walls as well as the excess plaster on top of the mold.

9 Use a metal scraper to scrape all the surfaces smooth and round the edges. The shape can be further rounded and smoothed with wet-and-dry sandpaper. Ensure that there are no sharp edges which would chip easily.

10 **The finished lump mold**
Leave the mold to dry (see p.79). Note that it has an undercut under the walls which forms the stem foot for the mold, raising it higher up. This makes it easier to trim clay off the mold and makes the mold easier to pick up when it is upside-down.

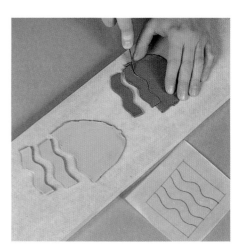

11 **Colored clay pattern**
Make thin slabs of colored clay (see p.78). The dishes are intended to coordinate with the tray made in the previous project, so make the shapes following the tracing paper pattern used for the incised pattern on the lump mold for the tray. Don't let the clay shapes dry out.

12 Roll out a slab 3/16 in. (5 mm.) thick from 2 lbs. (900 g.) of soft white stoneware clay. Do not allow it to dry, as it must bond with the colored shapes. Place the soft colored clay shapes on top of the mold, taking care when positioning them, and brush water on the top surfaces.

13 **Pressing the dish**
Do not allow the colored shapes to dry at all, but immediately place the soft slab of white stoneware clay centrally on top, taking care not to move the colored clay shapes. Press the slab onto the mold and push the clay up to the corners of the shape, as shown on page 90.

14 Roll over the slab with a rolling pin to flatten the surface. Even the sides can be flattened with the rolling pin. Then smooth the entire surface with a rubber scraper.

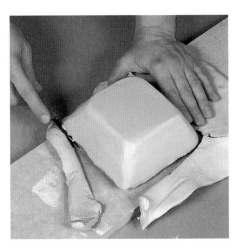

15 Trim off the excess clay with a potter's knife, running the knife blade along the undercut shape on the lump mold to give you a guide for a straight, even edge. Then smooth over the cut edges with a wet finger or template to round them. Small slab feet or handles can be joined on at this stage if desired.

16 **Removing the dish from the mold**
As soon as the pot releases from the mold it must be removed. If left on the mold past the leatherhard stage the pot will crack at the edges when the clay dries and shrinks. Place the dish upside-down to help the shape to dry more evenly than if it were sitting on its base.

After bisque (biscuit) firing to 2012°F (1100°C), the bases of the dishes were waxed. Then the dishes were dipped into transparent stoneware glaze and the bases sponged clean of any drops of glaze before firing to 2336°F (1280°C). The dishes were designed to fit into the tray made in the previous project.

Shaping soft clay as it spins on a wheel is a pleasure. Enjoying the process and learning from the making, as with all clay work, is more important than the actual pot made. Gaining the skills to make well thrown forms does not happen over night.

Success or failure is directly related to whether the learning is approached as enjoyable fun, or frustrating hard work. If you find yourself becoming tense and angry, stop and relax. Remember that it is important to breathe when throwing.

It is difficult to divide throwing into separate steps because it is a flowing process. This, coupled with the fact that there are many different ways of throwing, with very few potters using exactly the same hand positions, makes it especially important for beginners to search out live throwing examples wherever possible—whether in classes, or even on video.

Going to potteries and buying hand-made ceramics opens a wide opportunity for learning, firstly from the potters themselves, and then you will learn about the pots as you live with them in your own home. The experience of using a good, hand-made pouring jug speaks volumes.

Two points to remember when throwing: always use extremely well prepared soft clay; and always apply pressure slowly and evenly to the spinning clay, complete the shaping movement then release pressure slowly and evenly to take your hands away.

It helps to weigh the clay to the same size lumps for throwing. Prepare at least a dozen lumps of clay at a time (placing them into a lidded bucket to prevent them drying). Throwing the same shape repeatedly from weighed clay will give a better understanding of the shape and how to make it.

When the thrown pot has dried to leatherhard it can be 'turned' on the wheel. For turning it is essential that the pots are not too soft (as the shape will distort), nor too dry (as the clay will not shave off so well). Before buying a potter's wheel, experiment with as many types as possible to find the one most comfortable.

Above: Sheila Casson *"Salt glazed" Teapot, thrown and altered shape, blue slip applied.*
Top left: Jonathan Keep *Coffee pot. Semi-porcelain clay, thrown with slips brushed on.*

Michael Casson O.B.E.
"Salt glazed" Jug. Thrown with pulled spout and handle, slip decoration combed through with cut rubber scraper.

John Jelfs
Teapot. Dorset stoneware clay, thrown with impressed detail.

THROWING AND TURNING

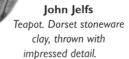

Emanuel Cooper
"Jug Boat." Porcelain, thrown and modeled shape, slab handle and spout.

Asa Hellman
"Zig-Zag." Stoneware clay, slab plate with thrown rim, slip applied over wax resist.

MATERIALS

12 1½ lb. (675 g.) lumps of soft well-prepared white stoneware (see pp.10–13)

Water

12-in. (30 cm.) square of thin muslin cloth

Candle or paraffin wax

Transparent or white stoneware glaze

Cobalt blue glaze mix

TOOLS

Sponge

Flexible metal kidney scraper

Folded strip of plastic in a 1½ in. (35 mm.) film container

Cutting wire

Turning tool (see pp.8 and 9)

Home-made plastic tool (optional)

Patterned "roulette wheel" (optional)

Brush for wax

Brush for applying cobalt mix

EQUIPMENT

Scales to weigh the clay

Lidded bucket

Throwing wheel

Flat boards

Thermostatic wax melter

Banding wheel

Kiln

Rubber gloves

Firing cones 03 and 7, 8, 9, 10

FURTHER INFORMATION

For explanation of unfamiliar words and technical terms, refer to the Glossary on pages 138–141

SOUP BOWL

This soup bowl, designed for domestic use, is a good simple shape for your first throwing session. It has a strong rounded rim and a sturdy wide foot, with a foot ring to grasp when dipping the pot in glaze. The inside shape is curved to fit a spoon. The wide, flat rim is not only a decorative device for dividing up the form; it also makes handling a bowl full of hot soup easier.

Hot wax has been used both to resist the base from absorbing glaze, and as a decorative resist to the cobalt glaze stain. When using hot wax remember that wax will catch fire if overheated. It is safer to use a thermostatically controlled heater. When using hot wax always take extreme care not to cause a fire, and not to spill it on anyone! Apart from the fire hazard, another drawback of using wax is that drips on the bisque (biscuit) ware cannot easily be removed. The only effective method is to re-bisque (biscuit) fire the pot to burn off the wax.

1 **Attaching the clay to the wheel head**
Attach a lump of soft clay to the dry wheel head as close to the center as possible. Note that the clay has a smooth convex base which will prevent air from becoming trapped under the clay when it is placed on the wheel.

2 With the wheel stationary, press down on the clay to attach it securely to the wheel. Note that the clay is a symmetrical cone shape, which makes it easier to center than an irregular-shaped lump.

3 Apply water to both the clay and your hands. There must always be sufficient water to allow the clay to run smoothly through your fingers. If it dries while your hands are in contact with it, the friction will cause the clay to drag and twist.

4 **Centering**
Have the wheel spinning, counter-clockwise. Lean your left elbow on the edge of the splash tray for stability, and press your left hand firmly against the left side of the clay. Apply pressure into the clay, not downward onto the wheel head—which would rub the skin off the edge of your hand. Press your right hand down on top of the clay, then begin to slowly slide it down the right side.

5 Begin by applying firm pressure with your right hand, then gradually lessen the pressure as your hand slides down the side of the clay, so that by the time both hands are facing, you are applying very little pressure. Slowly remove both hands from the clay.

6 Apply more water to the clay and your hands then repeat steps 4 and 5. Note that the shape of the clay is undercut at the base to make a ball shape, which can be controlled more effectively than a shape that spreads out onto the wheel head. The undercut is formed by pressure of your left hand pressing firmly from a line running from your thumb to your smallest finger.

7 **Making the base**
Try to center the clay with no more than three repetitions of these steps. When your hands, resting lightly on the clay, are motionless and you feel no bumps, the clay is centered. Open it out by pressing your thumbs or forefingers into the center with the wheel spinning fairly fast. Have enough water in the indented center to prevent the clay from drying.

8 Beware of pushing down too far and making the base too thin. When your thumbs or forefingers have gone down far enough to make the base approximately ⅜ in. (1 cm.) thick, spread the base to the desired width by moving them to the sides, then remove your hands from the clay. If you want a rounded bowl shape, make the inside base curved, not flat.

9 Now "tension" the base (see pp.10–13). Press the base down firmly and move your thumb or forefingers from the center out to the side two or three times, taking care not to thin the base too much. This presses the clay particles in the same way that the clay walls will be pressed, aligning them so they can dry more evenly, and preventing S-shaped cracks from forming in the base during drying.

10 Apply water to the walls of the pot by placing one finger on each side of the clay wall and squeeze water down your fingers onto the walls of the pot. Then sponge away excess water from the inside base: water must *never* be allowed to pool up in the base, as this weakens both the base and wall.

11 **Thinning the walls**
Place the fingers of your left hand at the base of the inside with those of your right hand facing them on the outside wall, and join your thumbs so that both hands work as one steady unit. Press your fingers together to gently squeeze into the thick clay, then begin to lift the wall by pulling your fingers up together.

12 Always thin the right side of the wall with the wheel still spinning counter-clockwise, working to gain height rather than width. Continue pulling the clay wall up until your fingers reach the top rim, then slowly release pressure and remove your fingers from the clay. For both this and step 11, your right arm should be resting on the edge of the wheel or tucked into your side for stability.

13 **Shaping the bowl**
If you want a wide flat rim, leave extra clay thickness at the top and gently press the inside of the rim out just a little to divide the rim from the bowl shape. The centrifugal force of the spinning wheel always makes it easier to widen a shape than to narrow it.

14 When the height of the bowl has been achieved, shape the wide curve of the belly. Place your left hand inside the pot and push the walls gently out to continue the curve begun in the base, at the same time pushing more gently back with your right hand on the outside of the wall, thus preventing the shape from going too wide.

15 **Smoothing the surfaces**
When the bowl is the desired shape, you can either leave the throwing lines, or smooth the surface with a metal scraper, as shown here. Hold the scraper firmly in the right hand like an extension of your fingers, and push the entire surface of the edge up to the bowl's surface. At the same time, push the clay wall out against the scraper with your left hand.

16 Trim the excess clay off the base with a wedge-shaped pointed tool. It is important to undercut the shape, as this will help when removing the pot from the wheel. Leave an extra amount of clay at the base of the bowl to turn a wide foot ring after the pot has dried to leatherhard.

17 Smooth the inside of the bowl with a metal scraper. Hold the scraper steady against the top of the wall, then move it down to the center of the inside of the bowl, and remove it. In all contact with the spinning clay, you must apply steady, even pressure and avoid sudden jerking movements.

18 **Finishing the rim**
Remove any slurry and round the rim by *lightly* wrapping the folded edge of a strip of plastic over it. Do not press down with the plastic or the rim will become flattened. The plastic has been given a handle by putting one end into an empty 1½ in. (35 mm.) film container and snapping on the lid. This will prevent the plastic from becoming lost in the clay slurry.

19 **Floating the pot off the wheel**
Flood the wheel head with water, taking care that no water gets inside the bowl. Hold a piece of cutting wire tightly between your hands and press it hard against the wheel head as you slide it under the pot. Take care that the wire is pressed against the wheel head to avoid slicing through too much of the bowl's base.

20 Repeat this process until enough water has been dragged under the clay to make it slide easily. Slide the bowl onto your flattened hand, taking care not to touch the sides.

21 Carefully place the pot on a clean, flat, absorbent board. The floating off process will have left water on the wheel head, so before attaching the next piece of clay, scrape your metal kidney once across the central thin pad of clay to remove the layer of water and leave a thin layer of sticky clay. This is ideal for making a strong bond with the next piece.

22 Drying and turning
Dry the bowl to leatherhard. Center a 5-lb. (2.25 kg.) solid lump of clay to make a "chuck" (this can be centered in two sections—see p.117). The top should be flat with rounded edges the same diameter as the inside shape of the bowl. Place a thin muslin or cotton cloth over it, avoiding thick overlaps of cloth.

23 Place the bowl upside down over the chuck; the muslin will prevent the clay from sticking to it. Adjust the bowl until it is level on the chuck, which will automatically hold the pot on center. The bowl should fit snugly on the chuck. Turn excess clay off of the base.

24 Hold the pot on the chuck
While turning, press your left hand down on the pot to counterbalance the pressure of the turning tool and prevent the pot from being pushed off the chuck. This foot ring is being turned to make a rounded shape with an extra beveled ring just below the main foot.

25 Smoothing the surfaces
The turning marks can be left as an added feature of the bowl, or they can be turned off with a flat tool like a metal scraper. The surface can be additionally smoothed using home-made plastic tools (cut from stiff plastic, such as old credit cards) with carefully sanded smooth surfaces.

26 Rouletted detail
A rouletting tool can be used to add detail (you could achieve a similar effect with a ravioli cutter). Here a zigzag pattern is applied to the raised bevel turned just under the main foot ring. The rouletting is primarily decorative, but also serves to make a clear line to mark where the glaze will be wiped off from the foot ring before firing.

27 **Waxing the bisque ware**
After bisque firing the bowl, wax the base of the pot to resist the glaze. You can use candle wax for this. If the wax is brittle and flakes off the pot, add a half teaspoon of paraffin to two candles of melted wax. Too much paraffin in the wax will make it sticky. **Important warning: Paraffin will make the wax even more flammable!**

28 **Glazing the bowl**
Wearing rubber gloves, stir a transparent or white stoneware glaze, ensuring it is the correct consistency (see pp.16–19). Hold the bowl by the foot ring and dip the entire bowl into the glaze for two seconds, then remove it and drain it over the bucket. Dip the bowl in sideways, edge first, *not* face down, as this would trap air inside the bowl, resulting in unglazed areas.

29 **Wax decoration**
Wipe away any beads of glaze from the waxed foot of the bowl; wax any areas you wish to remain white for the decoration. Here a banding wheel is used, with the brush held steady while the wheel turns. A throwing wheel can also be used for banded decoration. Diagonal brush strokes of hot wax were applied on both the inside and outside of the bowl.

30 **Glaze**
Now band a glaze mix. Cobalt blue is used here. Banding the glaze mix with a brush will leave distinctive lines where the brush marks overlap. Take care not to go over the surface more than once to avoid applying too thick a layer of color or wiping away the glaze layer. Always test fire the glazes and colors before use.

After bisque (biscuit) firing to 2012°F (1100°C), the bowl was glazed (glaze made by adding 8% tin oxide to a ready-made transparent glaze) and decorated, then fired to 2336°F (1280°C). There is a characteristic speckling of the cobalt blue glaze where the wax resist was brushed onto the bowl, giving a "batik" like effect. The wax burns off during the firing, so the kiln needs to be in a well ventilated, unoccupied room.

MATERIALS

15 1-lb. (450 g.) lumps of soft, well-prepared white stoneware

Water

1 12-in. (30 cm.) square of thin muslin cloth

Stoneware glaze (see pp.16–19)

TOOLS

Sponge, and sponge on a stick

Flexible metal scraper

Folded strip of plastic in a 1½ in. (35 mm.) film container

Cutting wire

Turning tool (see pp. 8 and 9)

Home-made plastic tool (optional)

Hole cutter

Potter's knife

Needle

Brush

Rolling pin

Ruler or other straight edge

EQUIPMENT

Scales to weigh the clay

Lidded bucket

Water spray

Throwing wheel

Flat boards

Kiln

Rubber gloves

Firing cones 03 and 7, 8, 9, 10

FURTHER INFORMATION

For explanation of unfamiliar words and technical terms, refer to the Glossary on pages 138–141

SMALL JUG

In general tall forms are more difficult to throw than shallow, wide ones, so you may find this small jug shape more challenging than the soup bowl. Most pots thrown on the wheel begin either as flat, shallow forms or as cylinders, as in this jug—which could become a mug simply by leaving the spout uncut. The endless shaping possibilities make the thrown cylinder an important form to master.

Clay absorbs water on contact, and the longer it is worked on the wheel, the more water it absorbs. Ideally the entire height of a cylinder should be achieved with three "pulls" up, because if too much time is spent thinning and shaping the walls, they absorb too much water and begin to sag. It is also important to make the walls as even as possible by moving your hands over the clay slowly. Quick movements can result in thick and thin sections which will weaken the pot. If a pot collapses, it is instructive to slice through the length of it to check for thick and thin areas; this will provide valuable information which will help to improve your technique.

After the leatherhard pot has been turned, it is essential to lightly spray water on top and cover it with damp newspaper for 20 minutes. This will re-soften the clay, making the cutting of the spout less likely to cause cracks.

WARNING

If a pot has thick and thin sections in the wall there is a risk of the pot "dunting" (cracking) with the thermal shock of boiling water, hot foods or oven use. There is therefore risk of injury to yourself and other people.

It is equally essential that any pots intended for hot liquids or foods, or oven use are finished with a food-safe glaze that is applied to the correct thickness and is suitable for the clay, which must be fired to the correct temperature for the correct length of time. Check with the suppliers of the materials for this information. It is also essential that the handles on pots are strong and secure.

If you have any doubts about these points, do not use the pots for hot foods or liquids or in the oven. This applies to any shape – not just cups and mugs.

1 **Centering and forming the base**

Prepare fifteen 1-lb. (450 g.) lumps of slightly firmer clay than in the previous project and store them in a lidded bucket next to your wheel. Very soft clay is more prone to sag and collapse when throwing tall shapes. Follow steps 1–7 on pages 98 and 99 to center the clay and form the base. The internal width should be 1⅝ in. (4 cm.) Now "tension" the base as in step 9 on page 100.

2 **Thinning the wall**

Apply more water to the clay. Put your left hand into the pot with your fingers at the base, facing the right side of the pot. Push the fingers of your right hand up to the base of the outside wall, so that now the fingers of both hands are facing each other. Gently squeeze the clay between your fingers and begin to lift them up the wall of the pot.

3 Continue squeezing and lifting the clay wall. If the clay dries and starts to drag or twist at any point, slowly release the pressure and take your hands off the clay. Put more water on the clay surface, and sponge out any excess from the inside of the pot with a sponge on a stick, then resume the thinning process.

4 Continue to pull the wall up until you reach the top rim, then release pressure from your fingers as you rest them on the rim of the pot. Remove your hands from the clay only when all the pressure has been released and your fingers are only lightly resting on the clay.

5 Again put more water on the walls of the pot by squeezing a sponge of water over two fingers on either side of the wall. Sponge any water out of the inside using a sponge on a stick to reach in.

6 Put your entire left hand into the pot to reach the base and pull the wall up as before. Note that there is a bulge on the clay wall where the fingers of your hand are pushing the clay out just slightly above those of your right hand. Use the fingers on the outside to lift this shelf of clay up until you reach the top rim.

7 **"Collaring" the walls**
If at any time the clay begins to wobble, put water on the outside wall of the pot, then press both hands around the base. Gently squeeze the clay in and at the same time lift the clay with your hands, moving slowly up the wall of the pot until you reach the top, then release pressure slowly and remove your hands. This will re-center the pot and extend the height.

8 **Smoothing the surface**
You can leave the throwing lines on the surface or smooth them with a metal scraper. To smooth the surface, hold the scraper tightly in your right hand and press the entire edge up against the wall of the pot. Move up the wall of the pot with your left hand inside the pot, pushing the clay up to the metal scraper.

9 Curving the flexible metal kidney as you smooth the wall will help to give a gentle curve to the wall shape. If you want to divide the form, press the cut edge of the metal scraper into the clay to form a ridge above.

10 **Narrowing the shape**
The shape can be narrowed by gently squeezing, or collaring, the shape with your thumbs and forefingers or by wrapping the thumbs and index fingers around the form. When making the shape narrower it helps to have the wheel spinning a little faster.

11 To flare the top of the jug, place the curve of the metal scraper up to the top edge. The scraper should be held flat onto the clay at a polishing angle. Gently press the clay into the scraper with your left hand. The scraper should still be lifting the shape to prevent the form from sagging.

12 **Rounding the rim**
Wrap the edge of folded plastic lightly around the rim of the pot, taking care that the back edge of the plastic does not touch the clay. This will round the edge and remove any slurry which may otherwise dry and become a sharp edge when fired.

13 Trim excess clay from the base using a pointed wedge-shaped tool. The thick, round rim left on the base will make a turned foot ring later when the pot is leatherhard.

14 **Lifting the pot off the wheel** Dry any excess water off the wheel head, then hold your cutting wire tightly between your hands. Push it hard against the wheel head with your thumbs or fingers to ensure that the wire does not slice off too much of the clay base as you pull the wire underneath the pot.

15 Dry your hands thoroughly on an old towel; wet hands would simply slide over the pot and give no grip. Cup your hands around the pot and gently lift it off the wheel head. It can help to tilt the pot slightly toward you as you lift to prevent suction from holding it to the wheel head. Place the pot on a clean flat ware board and leave to dry, avoiding drafts.

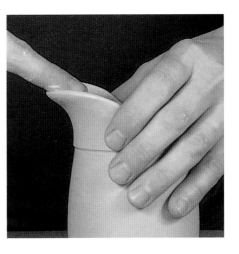

16 **Cutting back the spout** Dry the pot to leatherhard (see p.15) and turn the base (see p.102). Cut back the top of the pot to make a spout shape. Begin by using a hole cutter, not a knife, to cut holes where the shape of the rim goes down to a point on each side of the pot (a knife could set up a weak point which might crack). Cut around the rim shape with a knife.

17 Rub a wet finger over the cut edges to round them. A piece of stiff plastic can be fashioned into a home-made tool to further round and flatten the rim. Take care not to squeeze the pot out of shape while you are handling it.

18 **Forming the spout** Holding the two sides of the spout with one hand, wet the forefinger of the other and gently rub the end of the spout down. This will help to make the jug pour better. Do not press too hard or you may split the clay edge, causing a crack. Take care not to make the spout too thin, or it will chip easily when in use.

HANDLES

It is vital that a handle for tableware is joined onto the pot strongly enough for safe use. For strong joins, the clay must *not* be any drier than leatherhard—the softer the clay, the better. If the handles or the pots are drier than leatherhard when joining they will crack. Drying must be slow and even (see pp.14–15). Handles are not just functional; they can add detail and character to a form, so it is important to experiment. For example, shapes of soft colored clay can be rolled in for pattern. Study the handles on the pots you use, and make variations of your favorites. The joins of handles can also be made in a variety of ways; they can be smoothed into the form, which can make the handle join like the branch of a tree; or become a decoration in themselves, perhaps covered with a small detailed sprig-molded shape—there are unlimited possibilities to explore.

19 **Making a slab handle**
Cut a length of soft slab ⅜ in. (1 cm.) thick, ¾ in. (2 cm.) wide and 6⅜ in. (16 cm.) long. Put a clean dry rolling pin on top of the slab length and roll the edges flat while keeping the middle section of the handle thick.

20 Use a ruler or other straight edge to cut a thin strip off the edges of the handle to make them flat and straight.

21 Rub a wet finger and thumb over the cut edges to round them, then lift up the handle, turn it over and round the edges on the other side in the same way.

22 Decoration can be pressed into the clay. Here the edge of a ruler was pressed in twice to make two indented lines running the length of the handle. Trim the ends of the handle length into round semi-circle shapes.

23 **Joining on the handle**
Curve the handle into an S shape. Score a crosshatch pattern with a needle and wet the score marks where the handle will join the body of the jug. Lightly press the handle on the jug in the place where you want it, and then remove it. There will be wet marks showing you exactly where to score and wet the jug body.

After bisque (biscuit) firing to 2012°F (1100°C), the jug was glaze dipped. The glaze was made by adding 2% copper oxide, 1% cobalt oxide and 10% rutile to a transparent stoneware base glaze and fired to 2336°F (1280°C – see pp.16–19). Mugs were thrown from the mixed clays shown in picture 10, page 12, given transparent earthenware glaze inside, then fired to 2084°F (1140°C).

24 With the fingers of one hand inside the jug to support the wall, press the handle firmly onto the body of the jug to make a strong join, pressing from the inside to prevent the wall from caving in.

25 Attach the end of the handle firmly on the scored, wet marks, again ensuring a strong join is made between the handle and the body of the jug.

26 Drying the pot
To prevent the soft clay handle from sagging, prop it up with a lump of clay until it dries, inserting a piece of newspaper to prevent the clay prop from sticking to the handle. You can also prop the jug against a wall or solid object, using a piece of clay as a pad, again covered with newspaper to prevent sticking.

MATERIALS

3-lb. (1.35 kg.) lump of well-prepared stoneware clay

Water

White and black stoneware glaze (see pp.16–17)

TOOLS

Sponge

Flexible metal scraper

Home-made plastic tools for chess piece formers

Needle

Cutting wire

EQUIPMENT

Scales to weigh clay

Lidded bucket

Throwing wheel

Flat boards

Kiln

Rubber gloves

Firing cones 06 and 7, 8, 9, 10

FURTHER INFORMATION

For explanation of unfamiliar words and technical terms, refer to the Glossary on pages 138–141

DOORKNOBS AND CHESS PIECES

"Throwing off the lump" is a technique that allows small objects to be thrown much more easily than if they were made from individual small lumps of clay. Many people find it easier to center a large lump of clay than a small one, especially people with large hands. Try a 3-lb. (1.35 kg.) lump of soft, well-prepared clay – you may find that your hands have more control over it.

Trapping air inside a thrown form is a useful way to make shapes that would be too heavy, or cause the clay to "blow out," if they were solid. The trapped air prevents the shape from sagging, giving you an excellent opportunity to explore reshaping it without having to worry about the force of gravity.

Always remember to put a small hole in a hollow form at the leatherhard stage to allow the trapped air to escape, otherwise there is a risk of it blowing out during the firing.

3 **Trapping air**
Use a paint brush to remove *all* water from inside the pot. Then gently squeeze in the neck of the cylinder with the wheel spinning fairly fast. As you squeeze the wall in, take care not to push down at all because any pressure could cause the wall to collapse.

2 With your left index finger inside the pot, gently push the clay in with a lifting action to prevent the wall from sagging. This tall neck of clay is essential for enabling the top to be closed off to trap the air inside. The clay must not be too thin or it will sag at the shoulder of the form.

1 **"Throwing off the lump"**
Center the clay. Press your forefingers into the top and go down into the center of the lump by only 2 in. (5 cm.). Thin the walls to make a small cylinder, but leave the top thicker.

CHESS PIECES

Chess pieces can be thrown from solid clay if they are not thicker than ¾ in. (2 cm.) in any section. For larger pieces follow the steps to make them hollow. This solid-clay king chess piece has been squeezed up from the large lump of centered clay. The shapes are made crisp by pressing home-made plastic formers against the surface. Remove the finished piece from the lump of clay in the same way as the doorknob.

4 Continue to squeeze the neck in with the wheel spinning even faster as you close the top off to trap the air inside the ball form. Use enough water on the outside for the clay to run smoothly but do not allow any water to go inside the form unless you remove it before the top is closed off. The excess clay nodule on the top of the dome can be removed.

5 **Remove from the lump**
The trapped air inside the shape will prevent sagging even when you press down on it with a metal scraper as you work to smooth the surface. To remove the doorknob from the clay lump, use a needle to incise a deep line *well below* the form, then stop the wheel and cut off the shape with a cutting wire, taking care not to slice off any of the pot. Place it onto a ware board and repeat the process until you have used the whole of the clay lump.

After bisque (biscuit) firing to 1830°F (1000°C), the chess pieces are glazed in black or white stoneware glaze (the black glaze made by adding 10% iron oxide to a ready-made transparent stoneware glaze; and white made by adding 8% tin oxide to the transparent glaze). The glaze is sponged off the bases and fired to 2336°F (1280°C). The doorknobs (glazed with: transparent glaze + 10% yellow stain, 5% copper oxide for green; and the same mottled glaze used for the small jug), were glaze fired to 2336°F (1280°C). They need metal screws glued into the hole at the back to attach them to doors.

MATERIALS

1-lb. (450 g.) lump of well-prepared clay, any type, plus enough extra for a lid

Water

Colored decorating slip

Wax resist

Transparent glaze (see pp.16–19)

TOOLS

Sponge

Flexible metal scraper

Cutting wire

Turning tools

Brush

Roulette tool (optional)

Metal tube to make holes in lid

Rubber gloves

Glazing tongs (optional)

EQUIPMENT

Scales to weigh the clay

Lidded bucket

Throwing wheel

Flat boards

Firing cones 03 and 7, 8, 9, 10

Kiln

FURTHER INFORMATION

For explanation of unfamiliar words and technical terms, refer to the Glossary on pages 138–141

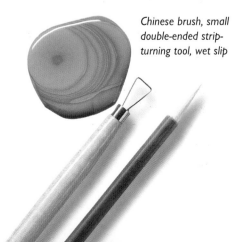

Chinese brush, small double-ended strip-turning tool, wet slip

TOOTHBRUSH HOLDER

Porcelain has been used for this piece, but any type of clay is suitable. Like the project Small jug (see p.104), the shape is based on a cylinder, but this one has a thick gallery lip at the top to hold the lid. When making lidded pots it is important to measure the gallery and rim of the lid carefully. Small amounts of clay can be turned off at the leatherhard stage to make a good fit, but you should make the lid as close to the right size as possible when throwing.

To make sure the lid will fit, it is best to fire it on the pot. This will prevent the shapes from distorting during both the bisque and glaze firings. When glaze firing the lid on the pot, it is essential that no glaze is on the gallery and lid rim, or they will stick together. Waxing the rims and base will prevent them from soaking up a layer of glaze, but even so there may be small droplets of glaze, which must be carefully wiped away with a damp sponge before loading the pieces into the kiln for firing.

1 Making the cylinder
Follow the steps as shown for the soup bowl (p.98) and jug (p.104) to center the clay and form the base of the pot. Begin to thin the wall of the cylinder by squeezing the clay between your fingers as you slowly lift the clay up to the top.

2 As your fingers reach the top of the cylinder, deliberately leave an extra thick top rim of clay. This will be needed to form the gallery for the lid to fit into. Always decrease the pressure of your hands slowly before you remove them from the pot.

3 The centrifugal force of the spinning wheel will tend to encourage the shape to grow wider, and putting your hand in the shape to thin the walls may widen the top of the form, so gently squeeze it back in to prevent it turning into a bowl shape.

4 **Forming the gallery**
The walls of the pot have been given a slightly rounded bulge to the sides and smoothed with a metal scraper (see step 9, page 106). Now form the gallery by pressing down onto the thick rim with your index finger. The gallery is being supported under the rim by the other hand: Keep it as thick as possible to prevent chipping in use.

5 Accurately measure the size of the gallery. Here a cut lollipop stick is being used as a measure. The lid will sit inside the measured gallery, with the rounded outer rim holding the lid on. Trim the excess clay from the base and remove the pot from the wheel (see steps 13 to 15, page 107).

6 **Making the lid**
Throw a small bowl shape with a thick rounded rim; this is the lid upside-down. Measure the rim to fit inside the gallery on the cylinder shape. It is always a good idea to throw more than one lid for any pot. They can be thrown "off the lump," as shown in the previous project.

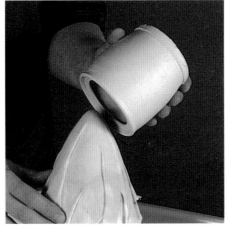

7 **Turning the pot**
When the pot and lid have been carefully dried to leatherhard, center a solid chuck of soft clay to a pointed cone shape and cover it with a thin muslin cloth. Try to prevent thick creases on the cloth because these could mark the rim of the pot. Place the cylinder over the chuck and turn the base flat.

8 After turning the cylinder, remove it and the cloth from the chuck. Apply water to the chuck and reshape it into a thick-walled shallow bowl shape, then skim off any surface slurry with a metal scraper and replace the cloth. Put the cylinder base into the bowl shape of the chuck and trim the gallery.

9 Turning the lid
With the cylinder still on the chuck, place the leatherhard lid on the gallery of the pot so that it is held on center for turning. Lids are such small objects that they would be difficult to turn if not on the pot.

10 Turn off excess clay from the top of the lid. The turning lines can be retained or shaved off with a metal scraper held at right angles to the pot (which will cut into the clay rather than polish it). The surface can be further smoothed using home-made plastic tools (see step 25, p.102).

11 Decorative rouletting can be added to a thin raised bevel if desired. This roulette wheel is an adapted book binders tool, which book binders call a decorative farthing wheel. You can make your own roulette wheels from plaster or bisque (biscuit) fired clay.

12 Slip banded decoration
As soon as you have finished turning the pot and lid it can be banded with slip. This should be done before the pot dries past the leatherhard stage. With the wheel spinning, hold a brush loaded with slip up to the pot and hold the brush steady until the pot has spun round to make a line of slip.

13 Wet slip can be given a combed pattern using a rubber scraper with tooth shapes cut from it. Alternatively, when the slip has dried to leatherhard you can cut through it, as shown here. If you do this, make sure you clean out the slip shavings in your wheel tray, as these will contaminate reclaimed clay.

14 Cut holes in the lid to hold the toothbrushes, supporting the back with your other hand to prevent the shape from distorting under the pressure. Allow the pot to dry with the lid in place. Bisque fire also with the lid in place.

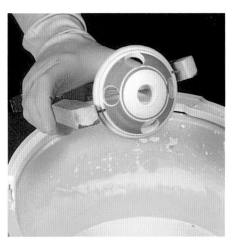

15 **Glazing the pot and lid**
After bisque firing the pot and lid, carefully wax the base of the pot and the gallery and the rim of the lid. You can use either hot wax or cold wax emulsion (see p.53). Wear rubber gloves and stir the glaze well. The pot can be dipped into the glaze with glazing tongs.

16 Quickly lower the pot horizontally into the well-stirred glaze so that it fills with glaze as it is pushed in. If the pot goes into the glaze rim first there will be trapped air inside, resulting in unglazed areas. The whole pot should be dipped into the glaze and removed within two or three seconds, then held upside-down to allow all of the glaze to drain out.

17 Re-stir the glaze, then hold the lid by its edges, with glazing tongs, and dip it into the glaze for two seconds.

The lid was fired on the pot; the gallery was clean of glaze so they did not stick together. If the lid is stuck on, place a cloth over the lid (to absorb the shock) and gently hit the lid with a wooden rolling pin to dislodge the lid from the pot. This pot had been bisque (biscuit) fired to 2012°F (1100°C) and glaze fired to 2336°F (1280°C).

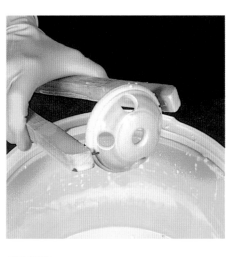

18 Hold the freshly glazed pots over the glaze container until they have stopped dripping. Carefully sponge any droplets of glaze off the base of the pot and the gallery and rim of the lid. Even the smallest drop of glaze will glue a lid firmly down, or cause the base of the pot to stick to the kiln shelf.

MATERIALS

2 5-lb. (2.25 kg.) and 1-lb. (450 g.) lumps
of well-prepared clay

Water

Colored decorating slips

Latex resist

Newspaper

Transparent glaze (see pp.16–19)

TOOLS

Sponge

Flexible metal scraper

Needle

Cutting wire

Turning tools

Brush and soap

Roulette tool (optional)

Slip trailers

EQUIPMENT

Rubber gloves

Scales to weigh the clay

Lidded bucket

Throwing wheel

Flat throwing bats

Banding wheel (optional as throwing
wheel can substitute)

Kiln

Firing cones 06 and 03, 02, 01, 1

FURTHER INFORMATION

For explanation of unfamiliar words and
technical terms, refer to the Glossary on
pages 138–141

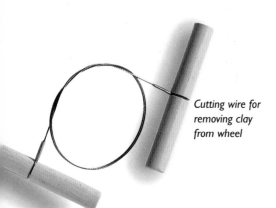

*Cutting wire for
removing clay
from wheel*

COMMEMORATIVE PLATE

Plates are well suited for throwing because the centrifugal force of the spinning wheel encourages all forms to go flat and wide. You may want to begin by making smaller plates, but do not shy away from large ones; they are not much more difficult to make.

This plate has an outer foot ring, turned – like the one on page 102 – and an additional foot ring in the center of the base, the size and shape of the decorative rim on the face of the plate. This inner foot prevents the center from sagging during the firing.

When cutting out the paper pattern, note that the butterfly shapes on the rim are both positive and negative. If you cut the paper carefully you can use both the inner and outer parts, thus achieving two shapes for the effort of one (cutting through folded paper gives multiples of these). This balance of positive and negative also helps to create a pattern effect.

1 **Attaching a bat to the wheel** Center a 1 lb. (450 g.) lump of prepared clay (see p.9). Flatten the clay onto the wheel head by pressing it down firmly from the top.

2 Spread the clay to make a wide pad of clay approximately ⅜ in. (1 cm.) thick. Press your fingers into the spinning clay to make ridges in the surface of the pad of clay. These ridges and troughs create suction between the clay and the wooden bat when it is pressed on top of the pad of clay, securing it on the wheel head.

3 The throwing bat should be dry. If it is wet it is more likely to slide on the soft clay pad. Place the bat centrally onto the clay, then with the wheel spinning, hammer your fist down exactly on the center of the bat to firmly attach it to the wheel head. Do not hammer down to one side, as the bat will not be level, and the rims on the thrown ware would be uneven.

4 **Centering larger amounts of clay**
Center a 5 lb. (2.25 kg.) lump of clay (see p.99). If you find this too much clay to handle, begin with a smaller amount and add clay to it to build the final centered clay weight up to 10 lbs. (4.5 kg.). Remove the top layer of slurry with a metal kidney before the next piece of clay goes on top.

5 Stop the wheel and place another 5 lb. (2.25 kg.) lump of clay on top of the first. Note that the base of the clay to be joined on must be smooth and convex to prevent any air from being trapped between the clay lumps. Press this top lump of clay down firmly to make a strong join to the clay underneath.

6 Put water on the clay and spin at moderate speed, centering the top lump of clay by firmly pressing down on it while your right hand moves down the side of the lump. The bottom piece of clay is already centered so you need only work on the top lump. Smooth the clay over the sides to make one continuous lump of centered clay.

7 **Forming the plate**
With water on the clay and the wheel spinning fairly quickly, press down on the lump. Lean into the clay, using the weight of your body rather than muscle power. Continue pressing down. If the clay becomes dry, slowly release pressure from your hands before taking them off the clay to get more water, then resume pressing down.

8 As the clay becomes flatter, take care that the edge does not form a rim that flops down, trapping air in the base of the pot. Pushing in the side of the clay as the lump is pressed down will prevent this.

9 When the clay has been flattened to the desired width, tension the base by pressing down on the entire surface of the plate as the wheel spins, moving from the center to the outer rim. Repeat this two or three times, but do not thin the base too much.

10 Normally plates have a flat, smooth area inside the rim, but to make this plate more interesting to decorate as a commemorative plate, a small ring of clay is pushed up to divide the center of the plate with an added decorative border.

11 **Checking the thickness of the base**
To check the thickness of the base, stop the wheel, and push a needle into the base until it hits the bat. Your index or middle finger should be pressing up against the needle down at the surface of the clay.

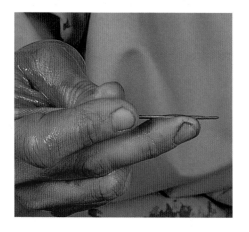

12 Remove the needle from the clay with your finger still pressed against it. The measurement between the tip of your finger and the end of the needle shows the thickness of the clay base. For a large plate the base should be ⅜ in. (1 cm.) thick. This will allow the cutting wire to curve slightly when it is pulled under the plate, and cut off extra clay from the center of the bottom.

13 **Shaping the rim**
After pressing the base to the correct thickness, the rim of the pot can be shaped. Here the rim is being pulled out to flatten it. Alternatively it can be thrown up like a cylinder and pushed over to flatten the shape. A metal scraper can now be used to smooth over the plate and the flat rim unless you want to retain the throwing lines.

14 Use a wedge-shaped pointed tool to remove excess clay from the base and more importantly to slightly undercut the base of the pot. This will make it much easier to get the cutting wire around the base of the plate; otherwise you risk slicing off too much of the base.

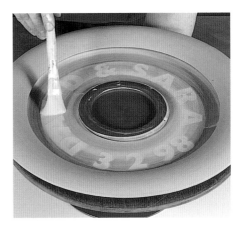

15 **Remove the bat from the wheel**

Use a strong flat tool such as an old metal butter knife to lever the bat off the wheel, making small movements on all sides of the bat. If it were levered off in one sudden movement there would be a risk of the rim distorting in shape. Pick up the bat and place it on a flat surface. A cutting wire must then be pulled under the plate before the clay dries. Take care to press the wire down hard to avoid slicing off too much of the base.

16 **Paper resist letters**

When the plate has dried to leatherhard and its base has been turned (see p. 102), dip paper letters and numbers into water and place them on the leatherhard clay with their edges smoothed down. These letters were printed out from a computer onto absorbent recycled typing paper and then cut out with scissors. You can also trace letters from books or magazines onto absorbent paper such as newsprint.

17 **First layer of slip**

Make sure the paper letters are attached well to the surface of the clay with all of the edges smoothed down to prevent the slip going under the edges of the paper. Paint latex resist onto the inner rim of the plate and let it dry (see p.36). With the plate spinning slowly on a banding wheel (or throwing wheel), band light blue slip over the outer rim and over the area with the names and date.

18 Band yellow slip in the center of the plate. Do not brush over the same area more than once or the clay will start to mix with the slip and muddy the color. Let the yellow slip dry, then apply a second layer to cover the red earthenware, creating a thick enough layer to prevent the clay from showing through.

19 **Paper resist decoration**

Cut shapes from absorbent paper and position them (dry) on the outer rim. The paper for the middle has been cut from a circle with the edges curved and additional shapes cut from the middle. Dip the pattern in water, shake off the excess, and place it on top of the leatherhard yellow slip.

20 Press the wet paper pattern onto the surface of the yellow slip, making sure that all of the edges are sealed to the surface.

21 **Applying the slip over the paper**
Brush or sponge dark blue slip over the surface of the inner circle. It is important to cover the whole surface right up to the edges.

22 Take each cut paper shape off the rim one at a time, dip it into water, and fix it onto the surface as before. Again it is vital to smooth all of the edges down well, but take care not to remove the thin layer of light blue slip from the rim.

23 Spin the banding wheel and use a brush to band the inner edge of the rim with yellow slip. Although the rest of the rim will have the yellow slip applied with a sponge, a brush is more controllable for the edge, and prevents any slip from dripping onto the central area.

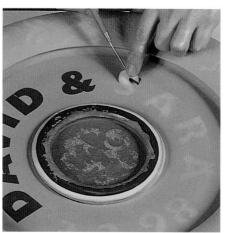

24 Sponge thick yellow slip on top of the paper resist pattern. If the yellow slip is not thick enough to prevent the blue slip from showing through, wait until the first layer has dried and sponge on another.

25 **Removing the paper resist**
Use the point of a needle to lift the edge of the paper letters and remove them, taking care that the needle does not gouge a mark in the clay. Throw away the slip-covered paper patterns before they dry and become a dust hazard.

26 Remove the paper shape from the center to reveal the yellow slip underneath. If the shapes have been cut from plastic, then wash them before they dry. The shapes can be re-used.

27 Use the point of a needle to find the edge of the latex on the inner rim of the plate and pull it off. This leaves the rim clean and ready to be decorated with a slip trailed pattern (optional). Once again the latex must be thrown away before the slip dries.

After bisque (biscuit) firing to 1830°F (1000°C), the base was waxed, and the plate was glazed by pouring glaze over the surfaces (see p.49). Transparent glaze must be applied thinly as thick areas will have air bubbles that make the glaze look milky – also thick glazes are more prone to crazing. It was then glaze fired to 2084°F (1140°C).

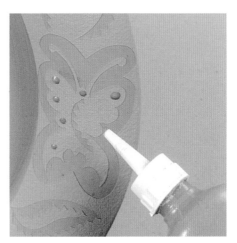

28 Use the needle point again to lift the edge of the pattern pieces on the rim and remove them. Don't let the clay and slip dry too much or the paper will stick to it and leave a thin layer of paper which is difficult to remove.

29 **Finishing touches**
When all of the paper resist pieces are removed, the pattern will show, and you can add more detail with a slip trailer. Use a trailer full of yellow slip first to apply large dots in between the letters. Before the slip has dried, take another trailer of dark blue slip and place a small dot in the middle of each yellow one.

30 Dark blue slip-trailed dots can also be applied to the pattern on the outer rim. These add detail and create a textural contrast between the flat surface pattern and the raised slip-trailed pattern. Take care not to apply the slip too thickly and do not apply slip on clay that is drier than leatherhard, because either will cause the slip to drop off or crack in drying.

CACTUS PLANTER

Thrown forms can be altered in many ways. An alternative method to the one shown in this project would be to cut the wall of the pot off and remove the circular base, then shape the thrown wall into an oval and place it onto a prepared slab of the same type of clay. Then cut and join the base onto the pot as shown in the cutlery drainer project on pages 68–69. This could produce square shapes as well as many others, providing an excellent opportunity to experiment and explore form.

The thrown "doughnut" shaped ring which makes the feet of the pot can also be adapted to make other shapes for both feet and handles. The thrown ring of clay can be flattened and the underside turned before cutting it to make flat rainbow-shaped handles. The diameter of the thrown ring can be large or small depending on the size of the pot. You can also throw a stack of foot rings or handles at the same time by dividing up a thick-walled cylinder with the shapes that can be separated at the leatherhard stage.

1 **Throwing the main shape** Center a 1 lb. (450 g.) lump of clay on the wheel and impress grooves before securing the bat on top.

2 Center 5 lbs. (2.25 kg.) of soft, well-prepared clay, and flatten the lump by pressing down on the top and leaning into it as the wheel spins fairly quickly. Make the base $5/16$ in. (8 mm.) thick after pressing it down to tension the base.

3 Pull up the thick wall to make a cylinder with a very thick top rim (see pp.99–100). Remove any water from the pot. Water should never be left inside a thrown form because it weakens the walls and can cause the base to crack when drying.

4 Make the walls concave shaped and then flatten the wide top rim. Trim off excess clay from the base and undercut the shape with a wedge-shaped pointed tool.

5 **Finishing the edges**
Round the outer edge of the flat rim by lightly wrapping folded plastic around the edge as the wheel spins at a slow speed (see step 18, p.101). The throwing lines can be left on or smoothed with a metal scraper. If you take care to finish the base at this stage you will not need to turn it later.

6 **Drying the pot**
Hold the cutting wire tightly between your hands and hard against the surface of the bat as you slice the base of the pot off the bat. If the pot is left to dry to the leatherhard stage without doing this it is likely to crack due to the walls drying and shrinking and creating tension on the base, which being stuck to the bat, cannot move and shrink normally.

7 Lever off the bat with a strong tool such as an old metal butter knife and let the pot dry on the bat. Before the top becomes leatherhard, place a sheet of plastic over the pot and put a clean bat on top of it. Flip over the pot by sandwiching it between the two bats and turning them over. Twist off the bat that is still attached to the base of the pot. Leave the base to dry to just softer than leatherhard. Wrap the plastic around the rim of the pot to prevent it from drying further.

8 **Making the foot ring**
Place another bat onto the wheel head and center 1 lb. (450 g.) of clay. Flatten the shape by pressing down on the center as the wheel spins fairly quickly. Press the clay out from the center to form a thick-rimmed doughnut shape.

9 Shape the ring of clay. You can score decorative lines into the clay as the wheel spins, or smooth it with a metal scraper. Use a strip of plastic folded over and held lightly on the edge while the wheel spins slowly, as shown here. Allow this to dry to leatherhard.

10 **To make the planter oval**
When the base of the pot has dried sufficiently to be picked up without distorting the shape, place it on a bat that has a thin layer of fine grog on it. The grog will prevent sticking, and help the base of the pot to slide as it is pushed to form an oval.

11 Cut a thin almond shape out of the center of the pot. Score a crosshatch pattern on the cut edges with a needle and wet these edges with water or slip.

12 Brush water onto the top rim of the pot and let it absorb into the clay to ensure the rim is soft enough not to crack when the pot is squeezed into an oval. Place your hands on the outer walls of the pot on either side of the cut-out shape, and slowly squeeze the walls together until the cut edges are firmly pressed together.

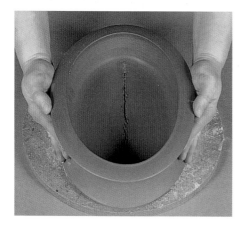

13 **Finishing the join**
With the pot now oval, the cut line in the center needs to be reinforced to prevent it from cracking. Use a modeling tool to press the join down.

14 Score a crosshatch pattern onto the join line using a needle wetted with water or slip. Roll out a thin coil of soft clay and press it into the join.

15 Use your fingers to press the soft coil of clay into the join. Smooth over the surface with a metal scraper.

16 Place a bat on top of the pot and flip it over while it is sandwiched between the two bats. This method of turning pots over prevents the shapes from becoming dented or distorted.

17 **Finishing the base**
Fill the central join line with a coil of soft clay then smooth it down with a metal scraper. You can leave the grog on the base of the pot or scrape it away with a metal scraper. If there are any sharp edges, round them by running your finger over the surface to press the clay smooth. Cut four feet out of the thrown foot ring.

18 **Attaching the feet**
Use a hole cutter to make drainage holes in the base, then round the edges on the cut holes by rubbing them with your finger or a wet brush. Do not press too hard, as this could push the base in and distort it. Score a crosshatch pattern on the feet and the areas on the pot where they are to be joined, wet all of the score marks with water or slip, and firmly join the feet on. Cover the pot lightly with plastic to ensure slow, even drying to prevent the joins from cracking.

After bisque (biscuit) firing to 1830°F (1000°C), wax was painted onto the underside of the pot in between the feet. The planter was dipped into a black made by adding 10% iron oxide to a transparent stoneware glaze (see pp.16–19, 49, 134). The feet were left fully glazed as the base was set onto kiln props placed closely together to fully support the base and to raise the glazed feet up off of the kiln shelf during glaze firing to 2336°F (1280°C).

MATERIALS

3 4-lb. (1.8 kg.) lumps of well-prepared clay plus 1 lb. (450 g.) each for sprig molds and clay for clay leaf shapes

Water

TOOLS

Sponge

Flexible metal scraper

Needle

Cutting wire

Brush

Hole cutter

EQUIPMENT

Rubber gloves for glazing

Scales to weigh the clay

Lidded bucket

Throwing wheel

Flat throwing bats

Kiln

Firing cones 06 and 03, 02, 01, 1

FURTHER INFORMATION

For explanation of unfamiliar words and technical terms, refer to the Glossary on pages 138–141

Rubber glove, metal scraping tool

TROPICAL PLANTER

Throwing large pots need not require much extra muscle power, especially if you use softer clay and center the clay in sections rather than all at once, as in this project. Most throwers, however, would center 12 lbs. (5.4 kg.) of clay in one lump, and you should try this as it may suit you better. The only real difficulty may be preparing this large amount without any air bubbles.

Sprig molds can be attached to any part of a leatherhard pot. Traditional "joke" pottery mugs had small frog-shaped sprigs applied to the inside of the mug – to be seen only after the contents had been drunk! If the sprigs have molded patterns on them, take care not to smudge them when attaching the sprig to the pot. You can press detail into the soft clay of the sprig after it has been securely joined to the pot.

If the plant pot is intended for outdoor use, read page 56 for advice on avoiding frost damage.

1 **Centering in sections** Center a 4 lb. (1.8 kg.) lump of well-prepared soft clay as explained in steps 1–6 on pages 116–117, then remove the slurry from the domed surface with a metal scraper before joining on the next lump. This has a smooth convex curve on the base which will prevent air from being trapped between the two pieces of clay when they are joined together.

2 Join the third lump onto the already centered clay and center this last piece on. As before, you should begin centering by pressing the wet clay down until it is well stuck onto the clay below. The wheel should be spinning fairly slowly until the worst of the wobbles and bumps are smoothed into the center, after which it can spin faster to help push the clay onto center.

3 **Opening up the pot**
Press down into the top of the lump with the wheel spinning fairly fast, then put water into the indented hole to prevent the clay from drying, and push down the center of the lump to open the pot up. Keep the wheel spinning fast to reduce the effort of pushing your hands down, and continue until the base is ⅜ in. (1 cm.) thick. Then tension base (see p.10-13).

4 **Collaring up the pot**
Put water on the outside wall of the pot and remove any water from the base of the inside. Place your hands at the base of the outside wall and press the wall in as you lift the clay wall up, moving your hands up to the top rim. This collaring up will re-center any wobbles that may have occurred during the opening-out procedure, and will also lift the wall, giving extra height.

5 **Lifting and thinning the wall**
Now lift and thin the wall. As your hands move up the wall, the left hand inside should be slightly above the right hand outside. Your left hand should push the wall out, creating the bulge or shelf just above your right hand. Your right hand lifts this bulge as both hands move slowly up the wall of the pot.

6 As your hands reach the top of the pot, decrease pressure slowly until you are touching the clay with no pressure at all, then remove your hands from the pot. Use a sponge to apply water to both the inside and outside walls, then remove any water from the inside base of the pot with a sponge – water should never be left pooled inside the pot.

7 Repeat steps 5 and 6 to thin and lift the walls higher. Take care to apply the right amount of pressure between your hands. When you begin to pull up the clay from the base, there is usually more clay to grab, requiring slightly more pressure than when your hands are moving over the thinner middle section. Apply less pressure as your hands move up the pot.

8 **Shaping the rim**
When your hands reach the top of their second pull-up on the wall, rest your fingers on the top edge and press the clay down to make a wide flat rim (or whatever shape desired). This should be done while the wall is still straight and relatively thick, otherwise the downward pressure may distort the shape.

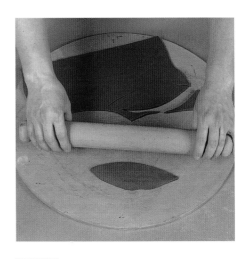

9 **Rounding the belly**
The third pull-up can give a round shape as well as a little more height to the pot. To make the pot rounder, the left hand inside the pot pushes the wall out more as both hands move up the wall. You can either retain the throwing lines made by your fingers, or smooth the surface with a metal scraper (see step 17, p.101).

10 **Finishing the base**
When the pot is the desired shape, finish the bottom edge. Undercut the edge with a pointed wedge-shaped tool and trim off any excess clay. The surface can be smoothed over with a sponge or round plastic template. A little time spent finishing the edge now can eliminate the need for turning when the pot is leatherhard.

11 **Clay-on-clay decoration**
Clay decoration can be applied to the surface when the pot is slightly softer than leatherhard. Make leaf shapes by cutting almond shapes from a piece of soft slab approximately 1/16 in. (2 mm.) thick. Use the rolling pin to roll the edges thinner. This makes the leaf shape thicker in the middle, tapering to the edges.

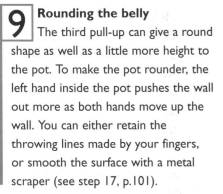

12 Re-cut the edges to make crisp almond shapes, then rub a wet finger over the cut edges to round them. If making several, put the leaf shapes on top of plastic and cover them to prevent them from drying out. Score a crosshatch pattern with a needle on the back of each leaf shape.

13 **Attaching the decoration**
Place each leaf in turn on the surface of the pot, draw a line around it with the point of a needle, then remove the leaf and score a crosshatch pattern in the corresponding place on the pot. Wet the scored marks on both the pot and leaves, and firmly press them onto the surface. Start from one edge, and gradually push the clay down to reach the other end.

14 **Making sprig molds**
Model the sprig shapes from soft clay. They should not be more than 3/8 in. (1 cm.) thick, and must not have any undercuts on the shape. Follow the steps shown in the project "Decorative Numbers and Letters" on pages 81–83 to make a cast of the sprig shapes.

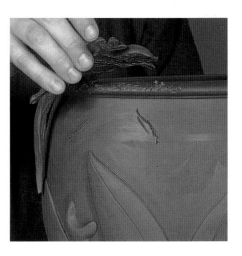

15 You can cast more than one small sprig shape at a time; these four small shapes will be on the same mold. Making plaster molds of the sprigs will let you quickly produce multiples of the same shapes, which can either be smooth or be given texture and pattern prior to casting.

16 Using sprig molds
Follow the steps on page 82 for press molding the clay into the molds. Do not allow the clay shapes to get too dry in the molds. If your plaster molds are dry, the sprigs may be ready to remove from the molds within just moments of having put the clay in. The softer the sprigs are when removed from the mold the better, as this makes them easier to join onto the pot.

17 Joining on the sprigs
Attach the soft sprig-molded shapes to the pot in the same way as the leaves (step 13). Clay shapes can be applied to any part of the form, inside or out, or on the rim, as shown here with the gecko shape.

The planter was bisque fired to 1830°F (1000°C) and could have been used then, but to achieve a richer clay color it was subsequently fired to 2084°F (1140°C). The planter was not glazed (a porous surface is healthier for plants). Glaze could be applied to the rim or other areas for decoration if so desired.

18 Finishing details
This gecko sprig was molded with a smooth surface, but after attaching it to the pot it can be given extra detail by pressing patterned or textured objects into the soft clay. A tooth-edged metal tool is ideal for making a zigzag pattern on the back and tail of the gecko. To make the eyes, attach soft clay and press it with the triangular point of a knife.

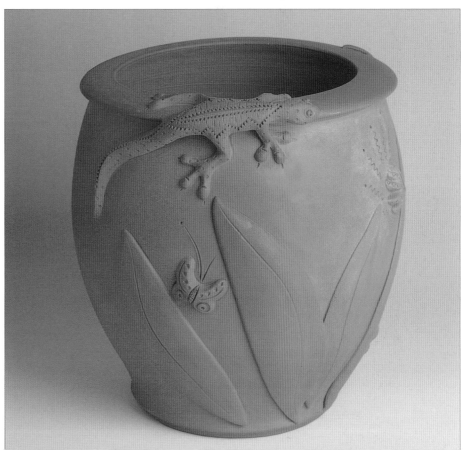

MATERIALS

15 1-lb. (450 g.) lumps of well-prepared
smooth clay

Water

4 oz. (115 g.) uncooked rice

Glaze (see pp.16–19)

TOOLS

Sponge

Flexible metal scraper

Needle

Cutting wire

Turning tools

EQUIPMENT

Rubber gloves for glazing

Scales to weigh clay

Lidded bucket

Throwing wheel

Board

Kiln

Firing cones 03 and 7, 8, 9, 10

FURTHER INFORMATION

For explanation of unfamiliar words and
technical terms, refer to the Glossary on
pages 138–141

GOBLET

Here is a project for anyone who enjoys a challenge. Goblets are difficult forms to throw in one piece. If the pot is wobbling when shaping the bowl, thin the stem section after the bowl is completed.

Another way to make a goblet is to throw a bowl, let it dry to leatherhard and when it is upside-down on the chuck after turning, attach a soft piece of clay and throw it upward to make the stem and foot. Alternately, the stem and foot can be thrown separately, attached to the bowl when leatherhard, and then turned. The stem itself can be turned thin, but the width at the top and base must be increased to give a larger surface area in contact with the bowl and foot. For the underside of the foot, the clay should be turned away from the center, to prevent this thicker, untensioned section of clay from forming an S crack when drying.

3 **Beginning the stem shape**
After two pulls up to thin the bowl shape, gently squeeze the solid clay under it to establish the stem section as separate from the wide supporting base. Take care not to thin this stem section too much or it will not be able to support the pressure of throwing the bowl on top.

2 **Thinning the bowl**
Thin the walls of this top section of clay as if it were a small straight-sided bowl with a rounded base sitting on top of a thick, solid lump of clay. The fingers of your left hand go down 1¼ in. (3 cm.) inside the clay, with the fingers of your right hand gently squeezing the clay opposite them to lift it slowly up as the wheel spins.

1 **Centering and shaping**
Center a 1 lb. (450 g.) lump of clay. Squeeze the clay above the middle. Press your forefinger into the top of the clay and push down by 1¼ in. (3 cm.).

4 Finishing the bowl

Continue thinning the walls on the bowl until they graduate from approximately ¼ in. (6 mm.) thick at the base of the bowl to as thin as possible, but leave a rounded top edge that will be comfortable to drink from. During throwing put enough water on the clay to prevent any drag, and use a light touch, as the stem support will tend to wobble if heavy pressure is applied.

5 Removing from the wheel

The surface can retain the throwing rings or be smoothed over with a metal scraper, as shown here. Trim excess clay off the edge of the base and undercut the edge with a wedge-shaped pointed tool. Put water on the wheel head, hold your cutting wire tight against the wheel head and cut off the goblet, ensuring that water has been dragged under the goblet to help it slide off the wheel. Dry your hands and carefully slide off and pick up the goblet by the stem and place it on a board to dry.

6 Turning and decorating

When the goblet has partially dried, place it upside-down on plastic to allow the base to dry to leatherhard, then put it upside-down on a cloth-covered domed chuck and turn the stem and foot. Lightly spray the bowl with water, cover with plastic until it has soaked in and softened the clay, and press rice into the surface to decorate it.

After bisque (biscuit) firing to 2012°F (1100°C), the foot ring was waxed and the goblet was glazed (see p.135). The green glaze was made by adding 2% copper oxide to a transparent stoneware base glaze (see pp.16–19). The glaze was applied thinly to avoid crazing. Where the glaze is thicker in the burnt-out rice marks, it is darker. The goblet was then glaze fired to 2336°F (1280°C).

MATERIALS

4-lb. (1.8 kg.) lump of well-prepared red earthenware clay

Water

Tin glaze (see pp.16–19)

TOOLS

Sponge and sponge on a stick

Flexible metal scraper

Double twisted cutting wire

Turning tool (see pp.8 and 9)

EQUIPMENT

Rubber gloves for glazing

Scales to weigh clay

Lidded bucket

Throwing wheel

Board

Kiln

Firing cones 06 and 03, 02, 01, 1

FURTHER INFORMATION

For explanation of unfamiliar words and technical terms, refer to the Glossary on pages 138–141

JUG

Capture the impression of the wet, spinning clay by retaining the fresh throwing lines; firing will "freeze" the movement, to give a hard fossil-like record.

When throwing a tall form such as this jug you will need to put your entire left hand and arm into the pot to reach the base. Wet your arm first to prevent the spinning clay from dragging on it. To keep enough water on the outer wall while throwing, hold a wet sponge with the thumb of your right hand and squeeze it to release water as your hands move up the pot. The sponge must not touch the clay, as this would remove fine particles of clay and make the surface gritty.

Pulling handles requires practice. You can pull the handles from the clay and leave them to dry hanging over the edge of a table in a curve before joining them onto your pot.

1 **Centering and forming**
Center 4 lbs. (1.8 kg.) of clay. After opening out the base and tensioning it, squeeze water from a sponge onto the inside and outside walls of the pot, remove any water from the inside base, and begin the first pull-up.

2 **Removing water from inside**
When you reach the top of the pot after the first pull-up, apply more water to the inner and outer walls of the pot, and again remove the excess water that has pooled up inside the pot. You can buy ready-made sponges on sticks (see p.8) or simply attach a sponge to the end of a stick with an elastic band.

3 **Collaring**
Collaring, in conjunction with pulling up the walls, will give extra height to a tall form. It will also re-center any wobbles, so if at any time your pot is going out of control, slowly decrease pressure from your hands, remove them, apply more water and collar up the pot back onto center. Take care not to squeeze in too much, as this will make the shape too narrow.

4 For this third pull-up to thin the walls, lift as you squeeze the clay upwards to gain as much height as possible. Aim to make a cylinder shape. If you round the shape too early it will be more difficult to make the pot taller, as it will grow wider instead of higher.

5 Shaping the pot
Pull up the walls again, but this time use your left hand inside the pot to push a belly out as both hands move up the wall. At the neck of the pot the right-hand fingers outside will need to overtake and be slightly above the left-hand fingers inside, pushing the neck inwards. The neck can also be collared.

6 Pulling a spout
Use your finger and thumb to gently squeeze and pull upward a small area of the top wall, aiming to thin the wall evenly without making the top edge too thin. A too thin edge may split when the spout is later pulled down and would chip more easily when in use.

7 Smooth over this thinned section of the wall by moving your index and middle finger over the clay from side to side. This will also round the top edge if you gently press the soft skin between your fingers over the edge. Note that throwing a thick top rim will help to provide ample clay from which to pull the spout.

8 Put the finger and thumb of one hand on either side of the spout, and use the wet index finger of your other hand, rubbing it from side to side, to gently pull the spout down. Be careful not to pull the thin clay down too far, as this could split it. Put your index finger further inside the pot and lightly push out a throat for the spout.

9 To emphasize the throat, hold the top of the spout between the finger and thumb of one hand, and press the sides of the throat in with a sweeping downward motion with the other finger and thumb. Try to make confident, bold movements rather than hesitant ones, as every time you touch the clay it will mark the finished pot.

WIRING OFF POTS FROM THE WHEEL

If you do not intend to turn the bases of your thrown ware, you can add detail when wiring them off of the wheel head. Using a double twisted cutting wire instead of a single smooth one when cutting off the pot from the wheel head will leave a distinctive line pattern on the base, and if pulled from side to side as it is moving under the pot the ridged lines will form a wave pattern. Twisted wires also help the thrown ware to release from the wheel more easily. Make your own cutting wires by attaching a double length of wire to a toggle on the wheel head with a piece of soft clay, then hold the ends as the wheel turns, so that they twist together. Fishing line makes excellent cutting wire.

10 Pulling a handle on the pot
Make an oval-sectioned oblong shape from soft clay with one thicker end. Score this and the place where it will join onto the pot, and wet the scored marks. Hold one hand inside the pot, pressing against the wall to prevent the wall distorting, and press the clay firmly into the wall to ensure a strong join. Smooth the joins and emphasize the oval section.

11 When the handle is still softer than leatherhard but has dried enough to make a strong join with the pot, hold the pot in one hand with the handle facing downwards. Put water on the handle, wrap your wet finger and thumb around the top of the handle and pull down, squeezing gently as you pull to thin and shape it.

12 Continue thinning and shaping the handle with strokes that start at the top where it joins the pot, and move down to the end. Have enough water on the handle to help your fingers slide over the clay easily. Try different finger positions to shape and thin the handle.

13 Finishing the handle
When the handle is pulled to the desired shape, press the free end onto the pot (if the pot is not too dry it will not need to be scored and wet first). The end of the handle can then be smoothed into the jug or given sweeping pressed-in marks with your thumb. Add a small dot of clay at the top of the handle to make it more comfortable to pour.

14 Glazing the jug
After bisque firing the jug to 1830°F (1000°C) it is ready to be glazed. Put on rubber gloves and stir the tin glaze well, ensuring that it is the correct thickness (see pp.16–19) and that there are no lumps in it.

15 Put the well-stirred tin glaze into a large, good-pouring jug, and pour approximately 2 pints (32 fl. oz.) of glaze into the fired jug, then immediately pour it out while you turn your jug around in a complete revolution. This will ensure that the glaze pours out over the entire rim of the pot and that no areas are left unglazed inside.

16 As soon as you have poured the glaze out of the jug, hold it upside-down and dip it into the glaze as far down as you want. You can push the pot down until it reaches the foot ring (providing you have enough glaze), or leave a portion of the pot unglazed, as shown here, to contrast the surface of the clay with the shiny glaze.

After dipping, a brush of glaze was flicked at the side of the jug to add a splash lower down. Where the glaze is thin, like on the rim, it allows the cinnamon orange color of the clay to show through. You can make tin glaze by adding 8% tin oxide to a transparent earthenware glaze (see pp.16–19). The jug had been bisque fired to 1830°F (1000°C) and glaze fired to 2084°F (1140°C).

DESIGN YOUR OWN

The many techniques shown in this book can all be adapted to suit your own designs. With the infinite possibilities that clay and glaze offer, it may be helpful for you to begin designing a specific piece which has identifiable sources of inspiration. Being selective can prevent confusion and help to give you clear direction for the development of your work.

SHAPE

Select the type of object you want to make and study the shapes and surfaces of existing examples. In this instance an ice cream dish has been chosen. Look for an object with a strong form which you can adapt and experiment with. Here a yellow squash on its side, as well as one cut in half, have provided strong bold shapes to explore.

PATTERN

A favorite garment or piece of fabric can provide an excellent reference for developing surface pattern or forms. Here a paisley print shirt was photocopied (including enlargements of the photocopies to increase the size of the shapes), and designs were then sketched as simplified variations of the pattern.

EXPERIMENTING

At the same time you're doing sketches it is important to be experimenting with the making processes in clay. Some ideas will be better suited to one way of making than another. Generally the technique that produces the shapes most easily will also produce the work better than other techniques. Throwing and turning has been chosen as the most suitable way to make this ice cream dish.

While experimenting with the thrown shapes on the wheel, sketches of the cut squash were pinned to the wall. These shapes blended with thoughts of ice cream

to produce an idea for a double-walled bowl which would insulate the ice cream and keep it cold longer.

The finished piece shown here was thrown as two separate pots. The outer bowl was thrown with the bulging ridges echoing the form of the squash. The inner bowl was given a smooth inside shape and a flat, wide rim to join onto the outer bowl (requiring careful measurements). To make the stem foot, the bowl was thrown with a solid base and then turned.

DECORATION

After the pot was assembled, the decoration was made by cutting shapes from newspaper, applying them to the leatherhard clay and sponging blue slip over the top before removing the paper. Then a slip trailer was used to apply further detail.

Use sketchbooks – or any plain paper stapled together – to quickly sketch shapes and ideas. Try to follow one idea through, considering many variations

on one theme by sketching what the form would look like—short and wide; tall and thin; with a thick rounded top rim or an elegantly tapering one; on a pedestal base or with a flat foot ring, and so on. The variations are limitless. Sketching is an invaluable tool for potters, as it is so much faster than actually making the pieces. By considering the variations on paper you can develop ideas to make more resolved, considered work.

EXPLORING

That is not to suggest that designing should only be done on paper, however, because that usually produces stiff, cold pieces of work which lack the qualities of the materials themselves. It is essential to spend time working with clay experimentally. Explore the nature of the material in all of its states of wetness and dryness, using all of the techniques and tools, and most importantly, the best tools available – your own hands. The combination of sketching and hands-on experimentation will produce pots that have strong design and clay qualities.

In addition to making sketches of forms (which can be as quick and easy as "doodles") it is also a great help to experiment with pattern, texture, and color. This can be done both on paper and on slabs of clay. Explore all manner of making marks on a surface: try anything from potato prints and charcoal rubbings of textures on paper to brush marks and getting the cat to walk across wet clay. This type of experimental sketching need not resemble anything. It can be done purely to enjoy the process. It will make you more confident when it comes to applying surface detail to your work, and you will develop your own vocabulary of patterns and textures which will become integral to your three-dimensional work.

Once you start on this exploration you will never again have a dull moment. Examining the objects that you are most interested in, whether flower or fish, architecture or airplane, will always pay off by providing a wealth of inspiration to draw from. If this goes hand in hand with on-going clay experiments, your work will be lively, interesting, and a joy to make.

Tutti-frutti ice cream dish with spoons
After bisque (biscuit) firing to 1830°F (1000°C), the base was masked out with latex, and the pot was dipped into earthenware tin glaze (see p.135). The slip has 7% cobalt oxide in it, which makes the color strong enough to show as blue through the otherwise opaque tin glaze. The spoons were fired on metal stilts so they could be glazed all over. The pot and spoons were then glaze fired to 2084°F (1140°C).

GLOSSARY

Agate ware
Ceramic made with contrasting colored clays or slip, named after the stone agate, which has striated pattern markings.

Alumina (Al$_2$O$_3$)
One of the main components of both clay and glaze. Alumina has a very high melting point of 3720°F (2050°C), which makes it useful as a main ingredient for BAT WASH.

Bat
A word used to describe different types of portable flat surfaces within the pottery workshop. Throwing bats are usually circular wooden disks used to attach to the wheelhead for throwing pots with wide bases. Kiln bat is another term for kiln shelf. Plaster bats are flat-topped dry plaster shapes used to dry and knead clay on.

Bat wash
A thin coating of material with a very high melting temperature, which is painted onto kiln shelves as a protective layer.

Banding wheel (turn-table)
Banding wheels have a circular top, usually 6–8 in. (15–20 cm) wide, which is spun around on a base by hand. They are used to apply bands of liquid material such as SLIP onto the surface of pots.

Bentonite
A clay made of very small particles.

Bisque (biscuit) firing
The first firing of clay which transforms it into porous ceramic.

Blow-out
A term used to describe the broken surface on pots after bisque (biscuit) firing if the clay contained contaminating materials such as plaster. In this book it is also used to describe the results of clay "exploding" during bisque (biscuit) firing if the clay was fired either too quickly or when still wet, or if it was too thick in sections.

Boxing
The stacking of pots of the same diameter rim to rim during drying and firing to help prevent distortion of the shape, as well as to save space.

Burnishing
The polishing of the surface of leatherhard to dry clay with a smooth hard tool (such as the back of a spoon) to give a smooth shiny surface.

Carbonized surface
Sooty carbon deposits absorbed into the porous clay surfaces during the incomplete combustion of organic matter such as sawdust.

Ceramic
Clay which has been fired to over 1115°F (600°C).

Chuck
Clay thrown on the wheel to make shapes to hold pots for turning. The clay can be soft and covered with a thin cloth, or it can be dried to leatherhard, which enables the pot to be put on the chuck for turning without the need for a cloth.

Cobalt oxide
Cobalt is a metal. Cobalt oxide is the strongest colorant within ceramics, giving blue colors. From 0.1%–5% will color glazes, and 1%–10% will color slips and clays.

Cones (pyrometric firing cones)
Cones are made in a numbered series which melt in sequence at set temperatures. The effect of the heat inside the kiln melts the cones causing them to bend over, thereby indicating the effect of the heat on the glaze or clay (the cones are made of the same materials as glaze). It is important to note that there are a number of different manufacturers of pyrometric cones, each having slightly different temperatures for their cones. The cone numbers given in this book are for Orton cones.

Coping saw
A handsaw with a U-shaped frame used for cutting curved shapes from materials such as wood. The blade can be removed from the saw and placed through a hole in the material and then re-attached to the saw, thus enabling shapes to be cut from the center, for example to make extruding DIE PLATES.

Cottle
A wall surrounding a shape which is to be cast in plaster. This wall holds the liquid plaster in place until it has set hard. Cottles can be made of flexible linoleum, lengths of wooden board, or thick clay.

Crazing
Fine cracks in the glaze covering a pot caused by the glaze contracting more than the clay of the pot. There are many different causes of crazing. It can be undesirable on pots intended for food or liquid, but can be encouraged as an interesting surface pattern.

Die plates
Flat shapes cut from strong rigid material such as wood, metal, or perspex, used to extrude clay shapes through (see EXTRUDER).

Dunting
A term used to describe sharp cracks in pottery when exposed to thermal shock. There are many causes of dunting, among them irregular thicknesses of the clay walls, incorrect firing temperatures, glaze applied too thickly, or glaze which is not compatible with the clay. If in any doubt, pottery should not be used for hot food or drink, or oven use.

Extruder (dod box or wad mill)
A strong metal tube that holds soft clay which is pushed down the tube by a metal plate through leverage or a corkscrew action. The clay is forced down through a shaped DIE PLATE to produce shaped lengths.

Firing cones—see CONES

Foot ring
A ring of clay forming the base of a pot.

Frit
Glaze material melted with silica to form a glass, then cooled and crushed into a fine powder. Fritting encases particles of material in glass to make them safer or less soluble in a glaze mix.

Grog
Clay which has been fired and then ground into different-sized particles from the size of sand to fine powder. The firing process shrinks the clay, so when grog is added to soft clay, the mixture will shrink less during the firing.

Glaze stain (clay body stains)
Metal oxides and carbonates (and commercially prepared compounds made from metal oxides and carbonates), used to color glaze, slip, and clay.

Kidney
A flat hand tool shaped like a kidney, made from flat steel, rubber, or wood (or home-made from stiff plastic such as old credit cards or the plastic tops of re-sealable food containers).

Latex
A suspension of synthetic rubber in water, used as a resist medium for decoration. Unlike wax, dry latex can be removed from the pot to enable further decoration before firing.

Leatherhard (cheese hard)
The stage of drying where the clay is no longer soft and "plastic," but is not dry and brittle. Leatherhard clay handles very much like leather or cheddar cheese.

Maiolica
Tin-glazed red earthenware decorated with colored glaze stains. Also known as majolica, though this can refer to specific pottery made from lighter-colored earthenware clay with multicolored glazes.

On-glaze
Also known as over-glaze. Very low-fired enamel colors which are applied on top of finished glaze-fired surfaces.

Opacifiers
Minerals such as tin oxide, which are added to otherwise transparent glazes to make them opaque.

Oxidation/oxidized
A term used for kiln firings to indicate that the atmosphere inside the kiln during the firing has plenty of available oxygen. This allows for complete combustion of the fuel during firing (using fuels such as wood, gas, or oil). Electric firings are always oxidized.

Paddle/paddling
A paddle is a tool, such as a flat piece of wood, used to flatten or shape soft clay.

Plasticity
A term which sums up the unique qualities of a clay which can make flowing shapes without cracking. The opposite of a "plastic" clay is a SHORT CLAY.

Pin-hole
A glaze defect which results in small holes the size of pin heads with rounded edges on the glaze surface. Pin-holing can be avoided if the kiln is "soaked" (see SOAKING) at its top temperature during glaze firing.

Props (kiln props)
Tubes made of a highly refractory material called sillimanite which remain rigid even at stoneware temperatures. Props are used to hold up the kiln shelves during firing.

Pug mill
A machine used to mix then compress clay into homogeneous lengths.

Raku
A Japanese firing technique which involves removing pots from the kiln when they are red hot and sometimes placing them into sawdust or other combustible materials.

Reduction
The atmosphere in the kiln when there is insufficient oxygen for complete combustion of burning fuel. The opposite of OXIDATION.

Refractory
Used to describe substances with very high melting points, for example, alumina, which has a melting point of 3720°F (2050°C).

Resist
A material which prevents a decoration medium, such as slip or underglaze color, from adhering to the surface of the work. Commonly used resist materials are wax, latex, and paper.

Ribs
Throwing tools often made from wood.

Roulette wheel
A coin-sized free-wheeling disk with a patterned edge usually attached to a handle (very similar to a ravioli cutter).

Rutile
An oxide containing titanium and a small amount of iron.

Saggar
A large slab-built lidded pot in which pots are placed during the firing.

Salt glaze
A method of glazing ceramics where salt is thrown into specially adapted kilns during firing. The sodium in the salt combines with the silica on the clay surface to create a glaze.

Setter
An unfired clay shape used to prevent a pot from distorting during firing. For example, a setter was needed for the cheese-dish lid (page 61) to sit on to prevent the walls from warping. The slab shrinks with the lid, thus preventing its dragging on the kiln shelf during shrinkage.

Sgraffito
A decorative technique where the surface is scratched through to reveal another color underneath.

Short clay
Clay which is not "plastic" (see PLASTICITY). A test to find if a clay is plastic or short is to make a small coil of the soft clay and bend it in a circle around your finger. If the surface is cracked then the clay particles have not slid and stretched over each other and the clay is described as "short."

Sledging
The use of a template to scrape around a solid lump of clay or plaster to form a shape.

Slip
Liquid clay, used for decoration.

Soft soap
A potash soap used to prevent plaster from sticking together during mold making.

Soaking
Maintaining a kiln at a specific temperature for a length of time.

Sprig
A thin-section clay shape applied to the surface of wet or leatherhard clay. Sprigs are usually made in plaster molds.

Surform
A hand-held woodworking tool rather like a cheese grater, available from hardware stores. Surforms are used to plane down the surface of forms.

Tensioning
To tension clay is to press the wet clay particles into alignment with each other so that they are lying flat on top of each other rather than in a random pattern.

Terra cotta
A gray or buff-colored earthenware clay which becomes an orange-red color when fired.

Thermal shock
A sudden increase or decrease in temperature. Thermal shock in ceramics can be caused by pouring boiling water into a pot, or removing a ceramic pot from a hot oven. See also DUNTING.

Tin glaze
A glaze which has enough tin oxide in it to make it white and opaque. Tin glaze usually refers to earthenware temperature glazes which are applied to red earthenware.

Turning
The process of paring down or shaving off excess clay from a thrown pot which has dried to the leatherhard stage. Turning is usually done on the potter's wheel, but open cylinder shapes can also be turned on a horizontal lathe.

Ware board
A term used for flat wooden boards which are used to put unfinished pottery on.

Wedging
The process of hand mixing lumps of clay until they are of a homogeneous softness and texture. Wedging also expels air bubbles from the clay.

INDEX

CREDITS

Quarto would like to thank the following potters who did demonstrations for this book: **Clare Finch** (slab and pinching projects), **Samantha Stone** (coil projects), **Pauline Monkcom** (plaster molded projects), and **Morgen Hall** (thrown and turned projects).

We would also like to thank John Leach of Muchelney Pottery, Langport, Somerset, for the inclusion of his work in this book. Special thanks also to all the potters whose work appears. All other photographs are the copyright of Quarto Publishing.

Quarto would also like to thank Bath Potter's Supplies, Dorset Close, Bath (01225 337046) for the loan of materials used in photography and for the materials used in the demonstrations.

Clare Finch

Samantha Stone

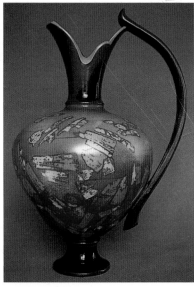

Pauline Monkcom

Morgen Hall